Audio Transcription Students' Book

Archie Drummond

Anne Coles-Mogford
Oxford and County Secretarial College

Joanna Gaukroger
Head of School, Business and Secretarial Studies
Gloucestershire College of Arts and Technology

McGRAW-HILL BOOK COMPANY

London · New York · St Louis · San Francisco · Auckland · Bogotá · Caracas · Hamburg
Lisbon · Madrid · Mexico · Milan · Montreal · New Delhi · Panama · Paris · San Juan
São Paulo · Singapore · Sydney · Tokyo · Toronto

Published by
McGRAW-HILL Book Company (UK) Limited
SHOPPENHANGERS ROAD · MAIDENHEAD · BERKSHIRE · ENGLAND
Telephone 0628 23431   Fax 0628 35895

07 084881 5

3 4 5 WL 9 210

Phototypeset by Gecko Limited, Bicester, Oxon.
Printed and bound in Great Britain by Whitstable Litho Printers Ltd., Whitstable, Kent

Contents

Alphabetic index to punctuation

Introduction

The aim of this Audio Transcription Course is to extend the typing skills you already possess and to train you to type business communications, in appropriate and mailable form, from dictation and instructions.

The course has been graded and so arranged that with diligent practice and critical attention to detail, you will be able to approach your Stage II audio transcription examination with confidence and transcribe business documents with conviction and self-assurance.

The operation of the transcribing machine is very simple and is easily learned. However, the ability to use the equipment efficiently to produce mailable documents requires intensive training and practice. Further, the training in transcription from the spoken word can be effective only if, before starting an audio transcription course, the operator can:

1 type accurately at 30 wpm;
2 spell and punctuate;
3 apply common rules of grammar;
4 form plurals, compound words and possessives;
5 arrange typing attractively;
6 listen carefully and follow directions implicitly.

As an audio typist, your job is to listen to the recorded dictation and produce a mailable document for each item dictated. In the early stages of transcription, you will listen to a phrase or short sentence. Developing your listening skills will increase your ability to remember words and will add to your memory span. Therefore, with practice, you will be able to type longer phrases and longer sentences without pausing. Expert operators, accustomed to the originator's style and trade terminology, can pick up and retain dictation fast enough to keep their typewriters moving continuously. These operators deliberately pace the transcription so that the typing is about a sentence behind the dictation. In this way, they can anticipate problems of spelling, punctuation, capitalization, etc.

Since the originator and the transcriber rarely have person-to-person contact, special instructions are generally dictated. The dictation might include identification of priority items, special stationery to be used, number of copies required, etc. In addition, directions and amendments may be presented in an instruction sheet which lists names and addresses of correspondents and any other information considered necessary for the successful completion of the transcription. At the beginning of each unit (from Unit 2) in your book you will find an INSTRUCTION AND INFORMATION SHEET for that unit. Always read this sheet very carefully and refer to it during transcription.

Some originators rely on the operator to look up and fill in details such as addresses, file numbers, references, etc. Such data can be found from previous correspondence, from files or from special reference books. Therefore, you should be well acquainted with the reference sources so that you can locate missing facts immediately. Of course, you will always have your English dictionary on your desk.

If you look at the contents pages, you will see that the first dictation (Unit 1) consists of very simple and straightforward short sentences. Your transcription moves from sentences to paragraphs, from paragraphs to headings and enumeration; then memoranda, letters, etc. As the course progresses, the work becomes more complex and demanding. You will notice that Unit 12 deals only with the composition of memoranda and letters from brief notes – this is an indispensable part of your course, and commands much thought and practice.

Employers suggest that the greatest impediment to an audio typist is uncertainty about spelling and punctuation. We all find difficulty in spelling certain words, and only by repeating the words in context are we ever likely to overcome the spelling problem. At the beginning of many units, there are sentences which contain words that you may have difficulty in spelling, together with homophones that you must be able to use correctly. If there are words that you spell incorrectly, make a note of them and type them every day until you can use them correctly in context without hesitation.

The audio typist must use the relevant punctuation consistently, and, with this aim in mind, we have included a section (in each of Units 2–9) giving guidance on when to use particular punctuation marks. You should read Section B in your book, paying special attention to the use of the marks and how they appear in the printed examples. In Section C of each unit (Units 2–9) you will be asked to type sentences based on the explanations and examples given. This will enable you to use punctuation positively and consistently in subsequent units.

The audio typist must also have a comprehensive knowledge of modern business expressions, and the office-style dictation concentrates specifically on introducing you to a wide range of current business terminology. The typing of the preparatory sentences, provided on the first page of each office-style dictation unit, ensures that you are conversant with any difficult spelling used in the dictation which follows. The more unusual business terms, and proper names, are listed in the INSTRUCTION AND INFORMATION SHEETS.

Remember that proofreading – checking your typing for errors – is vitally important. Possible answers to manuscript exercises and dictation in Units 1–9 and 12–16 are given in your book, and you should check your typing with the suggested answer before removing the paper from the machine. The answers to the office-style dictation (Units 10–11 and 17–20) are given in *AUDIO TRANSCRIPTION, TEACHER'S MANUAL*, and your objectives are: to follow instructions carefully, to manage your time effectively, to show common sense and initiative and to produce mailable documents (see below). Your completed office-style dictation transcripts should be passed to your teacher, together with your STUDENT'S OFFICE-STYLE DICTATION SHEET, for signature and/or comment.

It is possible that you will not always finish a unit in the time available. Therefore, you should complete the STUDENT'S RECORD SHEET (Units 1–9 and 12–16) or the STUDENT'S OFFICE-STYLE DICTATION SHEET (Units 10–11 and 17–20) at the end of a lesson so that you know exactly where to start in the next lesson. Copies of these sheets are printed in *AUDIO TRANSCRIPTION, TEACHER'S MANUAL*.

Any document which is not 'mailable' is not acceptable. By mailable copy we mean:

1   contents must make sense;
2   no omissions;
3   no uncorrected errors — misspellings, typing errors, incorrect punctuation, etc;
4   no careless corrections — if part of the wrong letter(s) is showing, the correction is unacceptable;
5   no overtyping;
6   no smudges.

In addition, the document must look neat and pleasing. The employer and the examiner will also consider the work in terms of 'output', ie, how much mailable work was produced in a given time.

In audio typing examinations the emphasis has moved to business production typing which requires a certain amount of thought and planning on the part of the student. *AUDIO TRANSCRIPTION* is a new course specially prepared to meet the needs of business and audio typing examinations.

Archie Drummond
Anne Coles-Mogford
Joanna Gaukroger

Dictating conventions

The amount of additional information or explanation that an employer will give to his typist will depend on:

(a) the type of matter to be dictated – highly technical matter and material containing unusual words may need more explanation – and the amount of display required.

(b) the capabilities of the typist.

In order to help the audio typist produce on paper exactly what the originator requires, certain dictating conventions are followed by most examining bodies. These are:

1   Full stops, question marks, colons, dashes, semicolons and exclamation marks are usually dictated.

2   The start of a new paragraph is indicated by the word 'paragraph'. In advanced examinations and in business, the paragraphs may not be specified.

3   Words to be underscored are dictated and then followed by the instructions 'underscore'; eg, 'Please send me details of your personal *(underscore personal)* computers.'

4   The solidus is given as 'oblique'; eg, 'The reference is TS/ *(oblique)* JT.'

5   Initial capitals are not usually indicated, but if there is a doubt, the following method is used: 'initial capital/initial capitals' eg, 'I have a current account with the *(initial capitals)* National Westminster Bank.'

6   When single letters need clarification, the Post Office phonetic alphabet is used; eg, 'Ask Mrs H *(for Harry)* M *(for Mary)* Green to see me.'

7   Figures are typed as explained in *TYPING: TWO-IN-ONE COURSE*. However, where it is necessary to distinguish, the word 'figures' or 'words' is used; eg, 'This is our *(word)* second visit to the theatre.' 'Please see pages *(figures)* 1 and 2.'

8   Instructions for headings are dictated before the heading, eg, *(centred heading, spaced capitals)* S A L E S   F I G U R E S or *(paragraph heading, initial capitals, underscore)* Typing First Course.

9   The 24-hour clock is dictated as spoken; eg, 'thirteen hundred hours *(typed without a full stop)* 1300 hours.'

10 Double or single quotes are indicated as follows: *(open single quotes)* 'Yes, send me a copy of *(open double quotes, initial capitals)* "Applied Typing".' *(close double quotes, full stop, close single quotes)* Some dictators may not state whether you are to use single or double quotes and they will just say, 'open quotes/close quotes'. Brackets (parentheses) are indicated in the same way.

11 Pounds sterling are dictated as follows: 'A cheque for *(pound sign eight point five four)* £8.54 is enclosed.' 'Please credit my account with *(pound sign oh point 67)* £0.67.'

12 If you are using open punctuation, there are no full stops in abbreviations. Even with full punctuation, certain abbreviations do not have full stops – see *TYPING: TWO-IN-ONE COURSE*. If for some particular reason the dictator wants stops inserted, he would say, 'capital letters N stop U stop R stop' N.U.R.

13 The spelling of an unusual word is given after the word has been dictated; eg, John Browne *(B R O W N E)* called to see you.'

Unit 1

A4 paper with margins of 20 and 80. Single spacing.

Exercise 1

```
She left early today.
He will call to see you.
They have sold the gold rings.
We saw her look at the new dress.
Fred will ask you to visit him today.
We will take her to see our new house.
```

Exercise 2

```
We will call to see you tomorrow.
They will see the old house on Monday.
I wish I could have been with you on Tuesday.
We will take you to see our new farm in Wales.
We look forward to hearing from you about your trip.
We will send your goods when we receive your cheque tomorrow.
```

Exercise 3

```
Thank you for your letter.
Thank you for your telephone call.
The train will be at least an hour late.
We must now look at the sales for August.
The account for May should be paid by 15 June.
The journey from Glasgow will be difficult in winter.
About 10 members of staff will report to your office.
We need additional information about suitable accommodation.
```

on headed paper please

<u>Subject to Contract</u> ← (CAPS)

ADDRESS OF PROPERTY: 59 Wightman Way Knowle Solihull B93 IRJ	DATE: 15 April REF: 3776/GRC
VENDOR: Mr Richard Smith ADDRESS: (in residence) SOLICITORS: Mason & Co ADDRESS: High St Chambers Knowle Solihull B93 OHU f ao Mr R Joseph	TEL: 056 45 44228 RESIDENCE TEL: 056 45 91115
PURCHASER: Miss Pamela Overend ADDRESS: please type in Miss O's current address Warner SOLICITORS: Addison, ~~Bewhurst~~ & Co Address: 130 Poplar Rd Solihull B91 4EW f ao Mr T ~~Warren~~ Warner	" 021-472 5560 " 021-705 6602

PURCHASE PR: £44,000 FREEHOLD

COMPLETION: to be agreed

DEPOSIT: none

REMARKS &/or SPECIAL CONDITIONS: none

CONDITIONS

Typist – fao = For the attention of

Unit 2

This unit is divided into 4 sections.

SECTION A   Six numbered sentences with words that you may have difficulty in spelling. Type the number and leave 2 clear spaces before typing the sentence. If you are not sure about a word, check in your dictionary. At the end of the sentence I will say 'full stop', and you must then stop the transcribing unit and type the sentence. Start to listen to the next sentence as you return to type it. Use A4 paper and margins of 20–80. Single spacing. Turn up 7 single spaces from top edge of paper.

SECTION B   In Section B, page 4, read the information dealing with the use of the comma. In Section C you will be asked to type sentences based on the explanations and examples given.

SECTION C

Exercise 1   Before I start dictation, close your book. Never look at the key while I am dictating. Six sentences will be dictated and you must insert the commas where appropriate: they will not be dictated. Each sentence will be numbered and, after typing the number, leave 2 clear spaces before starting the sentence. Use A4 paper and margins of 20–85.

SECTION D   This section will consist of short paragraphs about the spacing used when typing paragraphs in single and double spacing.

Exercise 1   Type Exercise 1 on a sheet of A4 paper. Use margins of 20–85 with single spacing. Commas will not be dictated, but you must insert them where appropriate. You will have to decide when to start a new line.

Exercise 2   Type Exercise 2 in double spacing on A4 paper with margins of 20–85. You will have to make your own line-endings. Commas will not be dictated but must be inserted where appropriate.

Unit 20
Office-style dictation

PREPARATORY SENTENCES

These sentences will not be dictated, and you should type them through at least once, paying particular attention to the spelling. The sentences are designed to help you with some of the more difficult spellings and points of English in the office-style dictation.

1 The accommodation is fully furnished and has a well-equipped kitchen.
2 The mortgage papers have been lodged with the Building Society.
3 Installation of central heating requires a sizeable sum of money.
4 The solicitor was advised to draw up the necessary papers.
5 He was disappointed with his friend's advice.
6 The old house had a unique atmosphere.
7 They purchased the self-contained flat adjacent to the office.

OFFICE-STYLE DICTATION

You are audio typist to Mrs G R Clark, who is Assistant Manager of the Knowle office of Booth, Cox, Winter and Co, Chartered Surveyors and Estate Agents.

Use dictator/typist initials and take a file copy of letters and memos only. Date memos and letters 15 April, 1986.

(a)

Letter of 85 words to Miss P Overend, 41 Grogan Road, Edgbaston, Birmingham, B15 4RZ
Subject heading: 59 Wightman Way, Knowle, Solihull

Accompanying manuscript to be typed on A4 headed paper.

(b)

Letter of 228 words to The Capital Building Society, la High Street, Coleshill, Birmingham, B46 3BW, to be marked for the attention of Mrs P Evans
Subject heading: Anchor Cottage, Grove Road, Henley-in-Arden

(c)

Detailed description of Hunt Cottages to be typed opposite sketches.

(d)

General description of 375 words of Hunt Cottages, 56 & 58 High Street, Hunt End, Solihull, West Midlands, B93 5HY

(e)

Memo to George Parkes, Assistant Manager, Solihull Office, to be composed from dictated notes.

Names and words other than those given above:

Mr R Smith	Forest of Arden
Mr Matthews	Harris and Sons Limited
cob	quarry-tiled
sagging	wrought-iron
collateral	copper cylinder
Saxon	blue pedestal wash-basin
	sole agency

RECOMMENDED TRANSCRIPTION TIME: 2½ hours

SECTION A   A4 paper.   Margins 20–80.   Single spacing.

```
1 Please let me have a video tape.
2 He must fulfil the promise he made.
3 It is my privilege to assist your father.
4 The accident occurred late on Monday evening.
5 A floppy disk is a magnetic recording medium.
6 I feel I have benefited from my holiday in Scotland.
```

SECTION B   Sometimes it is not easy to know when to insert a comma and when to leave it out, so today we will look at some definitions and examples. The comma is the most frequently used mark of punctuation. It tells the reader to pause and helps to make the meaning clear. Study the following explanation and sentences.

Use of the comma   NUMBER 1   Note the difference in meaning between these 2 sentences:
The clerk whom you saw last week has called. (no commas)
(WHOM YOU SAW defines the particular clerk.)
Now the same sentence with commas:
The clerk, whom you saw last week, has called.
(This implies that there is one clerk only.)

NUMBER 2   Use a comma after an introductory word, phrase or clause such as those starting with IF, UNLESS, ALTHOUGH, THEREFORE, HOWEVER, IN THE MEANTIME, AS A RESULT, etc. In the middle of a sentence, commas are placed before and after these words. Here are 3 examples:
As requested, we enclose our receipt.
Therefore, we need your help.
We shall meet, therefore, on Tuesday next.

PLEASE CLOSE YOUR MANUAL BEFORE THE NEXT EXERCISE.

SECTION C

Exercise 1   A4 paper.   Margins 20–85.   Single spacing.

```
1 The man, who was very ill, died today.
2 Mr Brown, however, must attend the meeting.
3 It is hoped, therefore, that you will be here.
4 Unless we hear from you today, we will cancel your order.
5 If we do not hear from Mrs Weston, we will call on you tomorrow.
6 Although she is retired, Christine still works for 3 days a week.
```

	Old Rate	New Rate
Breakfast	£3.40	£5.20
Lunch	£4.90	£3.80
Dinner	£5.20	£5.60
Tea*	£1.00	£1.20

Please rule table and insert leader dots.

* See separate circular No. F/24

SECTION D

Exercise 1   A4 paper.   Single spacing.   Margins 20–85.

Paragraphs are used to break up the writing into short passages
so that you can better understand the contents. There are 3 different styles of paragraph, but for the time being, we will deal
with the blocked paragraph where all lines start at the left margin.

When typing blocked paragraphs in single spacing, turn up 2 single
spaces between each paragraph which means that you are leaving
one blank space between each paragraph.

When typing blocked paragraphs in double spacing, turn up 2 double
spaces between each paragraph which means that you will leave
3 blank spaces between each paragraph.

Exercise 2   A4 paper.   Double spacing.   Margins 20–85.

As you have already learnt, in blocked paragraphs all lines start

at the same scale point.

You must turn up 2 double spaces between each paragraph when typ-

ing blocked paragraphs in double spacing.

You must fulfil your promise and send Barbara a video tape for her

birthday on 21 May.

It is my privilege to meet you at the station, but it has just

occurred to me that I am not sure at what time your train arrives.

Please let me know. Have you benefited from your holiday?

Unit 19
Office-style dictation

PREPARATORY SENTENCES

These sentences will not be dictated, and you should type them through at least once, paying particular attention to the spelling. The sentences are designed to help you with some of the more difficult spellings and points of English in the office-style dictation.

1   The month's expenses cheque was issued by the general clerk.
2   The absences had affected her work.
3   The annual budget was compiled from a variety of information sources.
4   The freight was always weighed at the depot and the total day's tonnage calculated.
5   Expenses procedures almost always require receipts as proof of expenditure.
6   He was not anxious to commit himself to a large weekly outlay.
7   Insurance on individual lives is known as 'assurance'.

OFFICE-STYLE DICTATION

You are audio secretary to Roger Gallier, who is a Director of Bowen Haulage.

Use dictator/typist initials (ie, RG/your initials) and take a file copy of all tasks, unless otherwise instructed. Date each task 23 January 1986, and insert extension number 26 on the letterhead sheet.

(a)   Letter of 201 words to E T Walters Limited, PO Box 24, 353 London Road South, Oldham, Lancashire, OL9 7HY, to be marked for the attention of Mr T Underwood
Subject heading: Weekly Contract to Felixstowe

(b)   Letter of 262 words to the British Overseas Trade Board, 1 Victoria Street, London, SW1 0HL

(c)   Draft advertisement of 75 words to be typed in double spacing.

(d)   Notice to all staff of 198 words.

(e)   Memorandum of 200 words to F Geeson, Accounts.
Subject heading: Annual Budget Preparation

Names and words other than those given above:

tonnage
Belgium
The Netherlands
Scandinavia
Yugoslavia
reimbursement of 'float'
Paul Daly Insurance Services
Mr R Tozer
HGV Driver
SPC switchboard

NOTE After the complimentary close in business letters, Mr Gallier always has his name typed as follows:

Roger Gallier
Director

RECOMMENDED TRANSCRIPTION TIME: 2½ hours

Unit 3

This unit is divided into 4 sections.

SECTION A
Use A4 paper with margins of 20 and 80. Single spacing. Turn up 7 single spaces from top edge of paper.

Six numbered sentences containing homophones will be dictated. If you are not sure about the meaning or spelling of a word, check in your dictionary. Each sentence must be typed on a separate line, and you should listen to a complete sentence before starting to type. Before you finish typing a sentence, start listening to the next one.

SECTION B
In Section B, page 8, read the information dealing with further uses of the comma. In Section C you will be asked to type sentences based on the explanations and examples given.

SECTION C
Before starting this section, close your book. Never look at the key while you are typing. Use A4 paper and margins of 20–85. Single spacing. Turn up 7 single spaces from top edge of paper.

Exercise 1
Seven numbered sentences. Commas will not be dictated, but you must insert them where appropriate.

Exercise 2
Seven numbered sentences. Each sentence will occupy 2 lines and it may not be possible for you to remember the complete sentence. Try to remember as much as you can and in phrases that make sense. You will have to make your own line-endings. Commas will not be dictated but must be inserted where appropriate.

SECTION D
The exercises in this section will contain main headings, subheadings and paragraph headings.

In Section D of this and future units, you will notice that you are given the approximate number of words in an exercise together with paper size, margins, spacing, etc. The originator of a business document will not do this, but you will be able to estimate the length of a document by checking on the number of units (recorded on a slip of paper by the originator) taken up by a particular piece of dictation.

To develop your skill in displaying exercises, look particularly at the number of words in an exercise and the amount of space it occupies when typed. Careful attention to this will mean that, later on, you will have little difficulty in deciding on paper size, margins, etc, when typing the assignments and when taking an audio transcription examination.

Exercise 1 (75 words)
This is about stationery and office supplies. Use A5 landscape paper and margins of 20–85. Single spacing. There is a main heading.

Form referred to in (e)

Please return to:

Typist – insert yr name followed by
" Secretary to K. J. Jordan, Harrison
Components, etc '

Name . _ . _ _ _ _ . _ _ .

Address _ _ _ _ _ _ _ _ _ .

~~Telephone number~~

I shd like to attend the farewell
presentation to Bill Palmer on
27 Sept. *

I regret th I sh be unable to attend. *

* Please delete as appropriate.

Exercise 2 (110 words)   This exercise will remind you about how to display paragraph headings. It has a main heading and a subheading. Use A5 landscape paper with margins of 20–85. Single spacing. Commas will not be dictated but must be inserted where appropriate.

Exercise 3 (112 words)   This is about business reports. It has a main heading, a subheading and paragraph headings. Use A4 paper and margins of 20–85. Single spacing. Commas will not be dictated but must be inserted where appropriate.

Exercise 4 (45 words)   This is a short exercise about buying from mail order catalogues. There is a main heading, a subheading and paragraph headings. Commas will not be dictated but must be inserted where appropriate. Use A5 portrait paper and margins of 13–63. Double spacing.

Exercise 5 (138 words)   This exercise is about successful business behaviour. It has a main heading, a subheading and paragraph headings. Commas will not be dictated but must be inserted where appropriate. Use A4 paper and margins of 22–82. Double spacing.

Unit 18
Office-style dictation

PREPARATORY SENTENCES
These sentences will not be dictated, and you should type them through at least once, paying particular attention to the spelling. The sentences are designed to help you with some of the more difficult spellings and points of English in the office-style dictation.

1 Jane was promoted from bilingual secretary to personal assistant after Mrs Smith's resignation.
2 The new machine was equipped with a device for collating papers prior to despatch.
3 He succeeded in making the acquaintance of the clerk.
4 It is necessary to allow access at all times to the library's resources.
5 In the preliminary round, they performed exceptionally well.
6 The company found it too difficult to fulfil the requirements of the contract.
7 The strategy had been to liaise with dealers and suppliers to improve sales.

OFFICE-STYLE DICTATION
You are audio secretary to Kevin J. Jordan, General Manager of Harrison Components Limited.

Insert references as indicated by the dictator and take a file copy of each task.

House layout is centred style with full punctuation. Use this style consistently throughout each task.

Date each piece of dictation 25 August 1986 unless otherwise instructed.

(a) Letter of 229 words to The Personnel Officer, GHI Computing Limited, GHI House, Putney Bridge, London, SW6 4JX.
Subject heading: Susan Caroline Jackson

(b) Memorandum of 231 words to Brian Fraser, Assistant Production Manager.
Subject heading: Replacement of Jigs and Lathes, Machine Shop II

(c) Press release of 336 words to be typed on plain paper.

(d) Memorandum to accompany press release, to Jill Wedderburn, Information, (to be composed from dictated notes).

(e) Circular letter of 162 words. Omit date, reference, name and address.

Names and words other than those given above:

Sheffield	Keith Wilkinson
Youle Brothers, Willenhall	Poyle Trading Estate
Geoff Goddard	Richard Waddingham
Birmingham	Bill Palmer
Slough	Edinburgh
Gloucester	John
Newcastle-upon-Tyne	The States

RECOMMENDED TRANSCRIPTION TIME; 2½ hours

SECTION A   A4 paper.   Margins 20–80.   Single spacing.

```
1  With practice you will win the race.
2  You must practise the keyboard drills.
3  The principal of the college is leaving.
4  I must say he was a man of high principles.
5  The car was stationary outside their house.
6  Order your stationery supplies from Mr Banks.
```

SECTION B

Use of the comma

We will consider further uses of the comma and, as we looked at 2 examples in Unit 2, we will now study the example in Number 3.

NUMBER 3   Words in apposition require a comma before and after; for example:
The Personnel Director, Mr Jones, will see you now.
Mrs Joan Black, Company Secretary, is in her office.

NUMBER 4   Use a comma to set off a clause that is not essential to the idea being conveyed by the sentence; for example:
Mrs Burns, who called to see you yesterday, is in Edinburgh.
My gold ring, which is of sentimental value, has been lost.

NUMBER 5   Here we see that the comma is used to separate indepen-dent clauses which are connected by such words as AND, BUT, FOR, OR, NOR; for example:
We thank you for your enquiry, but regret we cannot supply the goods.
I cannot send you a new dress, nor can I credit your account.

NUMBER 6   A clause starting with a participial phrase (the present participle ends in ING and the past participle in ED) is set off from the main clause by a comma; for example:
Having completed his work, the boy went home.
Planned to the last detail, the party was an outstanding success.

NUMBER 7   This says that the comma is used to separate a list of nouns in a series; for example:
We need more pencils, bond paper, carbon paper, and envelopes.
In June I am visiting Holland, Belgium, and Germany.

NOTE Modern writers appear to have adopted the American practice of inserting a comma before the conjunctions AND or OR connecting the last 2 elements, although this is not always necessary. If the last 2 words are linked together, then the comma must be omitted; for example: We ordered bread, pickles, and fish and chips.

NUMBER 8   Similar to Number 7. Use a comma to separate 2 or more consecutive adjectives describing the same noun; for example:
Miss Richards was a quiet, efficient person.
Peter Williams was a happy, bright, considerate lad.

NUMBER 9   Use a comma to set off names and words used in direct address; for example:
'These purchase orders, Miss Barton, must be typed today.'
'If you are asked, Mrs Thomas, say I have gone home.'

NUMBER 10   A comma is used to separate parts of a sentence that might erroneously be read together; for example:
A month before, the man could not have accepted the appointment.

DATE	TIME	FUNCTION	NUMBERS
Saturday 17 July	2pm	Wedding Reception + Barbecue	(120)
Friday 23 July	8pm	JTR Personnel Consultants Celebration dinner	(80)
Sat 24 July	7.00pm	18th B'day Party + barbecue & disco	(110)

uc

uc

Please rule table

NUMBER 11   Used to separate the 2 parts when the subject changes within the sentence; for example:
Marjory having agreed to propose a vote of thanks, the Chairman asked her to speak.

NUMBER 12   The comma is sometimes used to separate hundreds and thousands, and thousands and millions in figures; for example:
The gross profit was £2,250,000.

SECTION C

Exercise 1   A4 paper.   Margins 20–85.   Single spacing.

```
1  Whatever you wish, you may have.
2  Barry, the brain, knew all the answers.
3  Her bedroom was bright, airy, and clean.
4  Please bring sandwiches, coffee, and milk.
5  In addition to these advantages, the cost is low.
6  Our Managing Director, Mr John Baxter, is on holiday.
7  Bob wanted a new car, but he does not have the money.
```

Exercise 2

```
1  Passing your school the other day, I saw 2 lorries standing
nearby.
2  The leather chair, which is very old, is in your bedroom at
the cottage.
3  If you care to call on us, we will be pleased to see you any
day next week.
4  Therefore, please send us your order by Monday of next week
at the very latest.
5  Please send us your cheque immediately, or we will be forced
to take legal action.
6  In the meantime, I will continue to check the bank statement
for the month of August.
7  Mr Roberts, reports the Bristol store, is first in total
volume of sales for the past year.
```

SECTION D

Exercise 1   A5 landscape paper.   Margins 20–85.   Single spacing.

```
STATIONERY AND OFFICE SUPPLIES

The competent audio typist knows what kind of stationery to use
for each office task.  She/he uses not only paper but all office
supplies efficiently and economically.  It is good practice for
the typist to arrange her/his stationery drawer so that the papers
for the top and carbon copies are readily available and easily
assembled.  In other words, the most frequently used articles are
within easy reach.
```

Unit 17
Office-style dictation

PREPARATORY SENTENCES

These sentences will not be dictated, and you should type them through at least once, paying particular attention to the spelling. The sentences are designed to help you with some of the more difficult spellings and points of English in the office-style dictation.

1 The licence must be renewed in 12 months' time.
2 He accepted the accommodation which had been booked for him.
3 A membership card was acquired, to allow access to the club.
4 The au pair had been personally recommended by the agency.
5 Your co-operation is needed to ensure that the day's arrangements proceed smoothly.
6 The restaurant menu was up-to-date, with an emphasis on regional and foreign dishes.

OFFICE-STYLE DICTATION

You are audio secretary to Terry O Leonards, who is Manager of the Mount Royal Hotel, Preston.

Insert reference TOL/685/your initials on Tasks (a) to (d). Task (e) requires no reference. Take file copies as instructed by the dictator.

House layout is fully-blocked style with open punctuation. However, indented paragraphs should be used for work in double spacing.

Date each piece of dictation 7 May 1986 unless otherwise instructed.

(a) Letter of 299 words to Mrs R Y Tomlinson, 36 Parbold Drive, Ilkeston, Derbyshire, DE7 0UQ.

(b) Memorandum of 161 words to Mr W T Enfield, Head Office.
Subject heading: Brochure of Budget Breaks

(c) Memorandum of 122 words to W Freeman, Restaurant Manager.
Subject heading: New Barbecue Area – Patio

(d) Passage of 218 words, to be typed in double spacing.

(e) Promotion review form to be completed in respect of MARGARET SUSAN CARTWRIGHT. No file copy is required.

Names and words other than those given above:

John Howard
complimentary
refurbish
Forest of Bowland
Strasbourg

RECOMMENDED TRANSCRIPTION TIME: 2½ hours

Exercise 2   A5 landscape paper.   Margins 20—85.   Single spacing.

G U I D E   T O   T Y P I S T S

Paragraph Headings

These may be typed in capitals with or without the underscore.
Two spaces may be left between the paragraph heading and the first
word of the text which follows. Paragraph headings may run on
without spaces after the last word and if typed in lower case,
must be underscored.

If the text is typed in double spacing, turn up 2 double spaces
after the main heading and 2 double spaces between paragraphs.
If in addition to the main heading there is a subheading, turn
up one double between the main and subheading and 2 doubles after
the subheading before typing the first paragraph.

Exercise 3   A4 paper.   Margins 20—85.   Single spacing.

B U S I N E S S   R E P O R T S

PLANNING THE REPORT

The first step in planning a report of any length or complexity
is the preparation of an outline.

THE OUTLINE This briefly lists in successive steps the points
to be covered in the final report, but these points may or may
not appear as headings in the final report. Therefore, we can
say that an outline is a logical arrangement of the main and
secondary points.

THE TRANSCRIPT The audio typist should present the originator
with a clean transcript so that he may revise it or discuss the
draft with his colleagues. It should be marked DRAFT at the top
of the first page at the left margin.

Exercise 4   A5 portrait paper.   Margins 13—63.   Double spacing.

BUYING FROM A MAIL ORDER CATALOGUE

Home Shopping

MAIL ORDER All the largest firms belong to an

association which lays down codes of practice to

be followed by its members.

DELIVERY DATES If a delivery date is quoted and

not met, you may cancel your order.

Job 3   A4 bond and bank paper.   Blocked display.   Margins 19—88.

(44)
209 Bradford Street
(46)   LEEDS   LS4 5SP

Ref   FSS/IES

Today's date

FOR THE ATTENTION OF THE MANAGER — CLAIMS DEPARTMENT

Union Insurance Co Ltd
Calvery Street
LEEDS
LS1 3AE

Dear Sirs

POLICY NO 1789

I regret to inform you that a burglary occurred last night at the above
address.

The house was occupied at the time by myself and my family, and the
burglars forced an entrance through the kitchen door. We were not dis-
turbed so that we have been unable to assist the local police who have
been investigating the matter. However, I would state that all possible
precautions have always been taken to safeguard my property, and the loss
incurred was not due to carelessness or negligence on my part.

On the attached list I give details of the missing property, and shall be
glad to receive a copy of your official Claim Form.

Yours faithfully

F S Somers

Att

Job 4   A5 headed memo paper.   A5 bank paper.   Margins 13—90.

M E M O R A N D U M

FROM   J R Ingram, Sales Manager   REF   JRI/OP

TO   Mrs F P Slater, Supply Department   DATE   12 August 1985

TYPING: TWO-IN-ONE COURSE

Would you please confirm that Order No 1275 for 150 copies of Typing: Two-in-
One Course has been despatched.

Raybold Technical College, Manchester, who placed the order, require them
urgently for the beginning of the autumn term.

SUCCESSFUL BUSINESS BEHAVIOUR

<u>Use Common Sense</u>

<u>Remember names.</u> An important quality of a successful person

is an ability to remember names. You will be meeting many

new people, and they will be flattered if you call them by

name the next time you meet them.

<u>Watch others.</u> As a new member of the office staff, you need

to learn where to go for materials, how to arrange your work,

and what are acceptable office standards. You can do this

by keeping your eyes and ears open.

<u>Ask questions.</u> If you have a problem which you cannot solve,

ask questions. Your colleagues will be glad to help you or

to answer any intelligent questions.

<u>Follow the rules.</u> In your new job you will learn company

procedure and ways of dealing with situations that arise.

Suggestions for improvements are welcomed by businessmen but

only after you have been in the position for some time.

NOTE In the above exercise, lower case and the underscore were used
for the paragraph headings. If there are no specific instructions, use
whichever style you prefer.

A4 bond paper.   Single spacing.   Margins 19—88.

ANNUAL REPORT OF W. H. JOHNSON & CO. LTD.

At the 16th Annual General Meeting of W. H. Johnson & Co. Ltd. held at
the Registered Office of the Company in London, on Thursday 20 February,
Mr. B. L. Barrows, the Chairman and Managing Director, presided. The
following is an extract from his circulated statement:

'Ladies and Gentlemen, I welcome your presence at the Annual General
Meeting, and before moving the adoption of the Report and Accounts, which
have already been circulated, I should like to refer to some of the features of the Accounts.

'It gives me much pleasure to be able to report that the past year has
been a very satisfactory one in many respects. A continued improvement
has been made in the affairs of the Company as a whole, and this is revealed by the results in the Annual Report. There has been an increase
in the net profit before taxation from £2,557,465 to £2,906,146, which is
a record in the history of the Company.

'An increased contribution has been made by each of our various activities,
as can be seen from the Analysis of Profits shown below.

Analysis of Profits for 1985

	(38)	(46)	(54)	(62)
	1985		1984	
	£'000	%	£'000	%
Fish	990	25.0	839	26.5
Poultry	1,127	28.4	1,042	32.8
Frozen Foods ...	564	14.2	261	8.2
Other Foods	735	18.5	622	19.6
Other Activities	552	13.9	407	12.9
	3,968	100.0	3,171	100.0

'Our policy over the past 4 years has resulted in a strengthening of the
Company's position, and has undoubtedly contributed to its success. The
development has been concentrated mainly upon the Company's food interests,
86% of the profit resulting from the production, distribution and sale of
quality foodstuffs.

'I am happy to tell you that, in view of the increased profits, your Board
has recommended a final dividend of 6%, as compared with that for the previous year of 4%, thus making, with the increased interim dividend of 4%,
a total distribution of 10% for the year on the Ordinary Capital.'

The Chairman concluded his remarks by saying that the results for the 1st
quarter of the current year were even better than those for the same period
as that under review, and he felt confident that the profits for the current
year would show a further substantial increase.

Unit 4

This unit is divided into 4 sections.

SECTION A Six numbered sentences containing words that may be difficult to spell. Use A4 paper and margins of 20 and 80. You must type each sentence on a separate line, and you should listen to a complete sentence before starting to type. Before you finish typing a sentence, start listening to the next one.

SECTION B In Section B, page 13, read the information dealing with the use of initial capitals. In Section C you will be asked to type sentences based on the explanations and examples given.

SECTION C Type Exercises 1 and 2 on a sheet of A4 paper with margins of 20–85. Use single spacing.

Exercise 1 Seven sentences covering the use of initial capitals. Type each sentence on a separate line. Listen to a complete sentence before starting to type. Before you finish typing a sentence, start listening to the next one.

Exercise 2 Seven sentences covering the use of initial capitals. Follow instructions given for Exercise 1.

SECTION D This section will contain exercises with shoulder headings, side headings and sums of money in context. If you require further help on the typing of these headings, see *TYPING: TWO-IN-ONE COURSE*, pages 38 and 92, and page 42 for information about typing sums of money in context.

You are reminded about developing your skill in displaying exercises. Look particularly at the number of words in an exercise and the amount of space it occupies when typed. Careful attention to this will mean that, later on, you will have little difficulty in deciding on paper size, margins, etc, when typing the assignments and when taking an audio transcription examination.

Exercise 1 (150 words) This exercise contains a main heading and shoulder headings. It is a reminder about the importance of proofreading. Use A4 paper, margins of 20–85 and single spacing.

Exercise 2 (100 words) This exercise has a main heading, a subheading and shoulder headings. It is about booking hotel accommodation. Use A5 portrait paper with margins of 13–63. Single spacing.

Exercise 3 This exercise has a main heading, a subheading and side headings. Type it from the typescript layout given on page 16 of your book. This exercise also has sums of money in context.

Exercise 4 (160 words) This exercise has a main heading and paragraph headings. The reference books referred to in the exercise are: a dictionary, *Applied Typing*, telephone directories and the Post Office Guide.
Use A4 paper and margins of 20–85. Double spacing.

INTERIM

your Board has recommended a final dividend of 6%, as compared w th for the previous yr of 4%, thus making, w the increased interim dividend of 4%, a total distribution of 10% for the yr on the Ordinary Capital'.

The Chairman concluded his remarks by saying th the results for the 1st quarter of the current yr were even better than those for the same period as th under review, + he felt confident th the profits for the current yr wld show a further sub-stantial increase.

```
1  Mary Baker was a competent typist.
2  You must specify your requirements.
3  Please make the necessary arrangements.
4  Typing errors can have disastrous results.
5  The bird floated upwards on a current of air.
6  Paul had asked me to book extra accommodation.
```

SECTION B

**Use of
initial capitals**

Today I am going to give you some guidance on when to use initial capitals.

NUMBER 1   The first letter of the first word of a sentence and any expression that is used as a sentence should have a capital letter; for example: I heard you won the sales contest. Congratulations!

NUMBER 2   The first letter of a proper noun or an adjective derived from a proper noun should have a capital letter; for example:
Sally learned Spanish and typewriting at college.

NUMBER 3   Type an initial capital for each word in the names of companies, associations, committees, boards, religious groups, political parties, societies, clubs, etc, ACCORDING TO THE STYLE ESTAB-LISHED BY THE PARTICULAR ORGANIZATION.* Capitalize the T in THE as the first word of an organization only when it is part of the official name; for example:
The prize was awarded by The Steel Corporation.
Send to the Bank of Scotland for the leaflet.
(In this case THE is not part of the name of the bank.) The only way you can be certain of typing a name correctly, is to check with the organiza-tion's letterhead or in the telephone directory.

NUMBER 4   Use an initial capital in the names of government organiza-tions and national, international, county and city governments and their subdivisions; for example:
We visited the House of Commons.
Write to the Department of the Environment.

NUMBER 5   Use an initial capital for the first word and all principal words in the title of a publication. Capitalize the T in the word THE at the beginning of a title ONLY IF IT IS PART OF THE TITLE; for example:
I find the book The Reader's Digest very interesting.

NUMBER 6   Use an initial capital for the names of days and months; holidays; national, civic and religious feast days; for example:
We will celebrate St Patrick's Day.
We also have a holiday on May Day.

NUMBER 7   Type an initial capital for nouns followed by a numeral indicating order in sequence; for example:
You will find the answer in Book II, Part IV, Section 17.

NUMBER 8   Use an initial capital for specific geographical terms and points of the compass when they denote a region of a country; for example:
Unemployment in the North is up by 3,000.

*In numbers 3, 4, and 5 it is not usual to type initial capitals for articles, conjunctions and short prepositions.

ANNUAL REPORT OF W. H. JOHNSON & Co. LTD. ← u/score

At the 16th AGM of W. H. Johnson & Co Ltd. held at the Registered Office of the Co in London, on Thurs 20 Feb, Mr. B. L. Barrows, [BARROWS] uc/ the Chairman & managing director, presided. ↗ (run on)

The following is an extract from his circulated statement:
'Ladies & Gentlemen, I welcome yr presence at the AGM, & before JT ~~moving~~ moving the adoption of the Report & A/cs, wh hv already bn circulated, I shld like to refer to some of the features of the A/cs.

'It gives me much pleasure to be able to report th the/past year has bn a very satisfactory one in many respects. A continued improvement has bn made in the affairs of the Co. as a whole, & this is revealed by the results in the Annual Report. There has bn an increase in the net profit before taxation from £2,557,465 to
NP/ £2,906,146, wh is a record in the history of the Co. [An increased contribution has bn made by ea of our various activities, as can
uc/ be seen from the analysis of Profits shown below.

Analysis of Profits for 1985

	1985		1984	
	990	25.0	839	26.5
	£'000	%	£'000	%
Fish				
Poultry	1,127	28.4	1,042	32.8
Frozen Foods	564	14.2	261	8.2
Other Foods	735	18.5	622	19.6
Other Activities	552	13.9	407	12.9
	3,968	100.0	3,171	100.0

'Our policy over the past 4 yrs has resulted in a strengthening of the Co's position, & has undoubtedly contributed to its success. The development has bn concentrated mainly upon the Co's food interests, 86% of the profit resulting from the production, distribution & sale of quality foodstuffs.

'I am happy to tell you tn, in view of the increased profits,

NUMBER 9   Use an initial capital for the names of business departments and a person's designation; for example:
Mr Roberts, Company Secretary, wishes to speak to Kate Cross from the Marketing Department.

NOTE (1)   Do NOT use initial capitals for seasons of the year, names of decades and centuries; for example:
We have our holidays in the summer.
He lived in the eighteenth century.
She was famous in the late twenties.

(2)   Do NOT use initial capitals for words that were originally proper names, but have developed specialized meanings; for example:
Please order plaster of paris.
Use roman numerals when enumerating the items.

SECTION C

Exercises 1 and 2 on a sheet of A4 paper.   Margins 20–85.
Single spacing.

Exercise 1

1   Is Easter Sunday on 22 April?
2   I hope to see you on Christmas Eve.
3   He is a member of the Liberal Party.
4   Please order the book The World at Work.
5   He went to the Baptist Church on Saturday.
6   When I was in France, I met many Dutch people.
7   When on holiday, we will visit the West Country.

Exercise 2

1   Three new factories have been built in the South.
2   His talk was entitled Administration in Business.
3   Look in Volume III, Section 14, page 11 of that book.
4   I visited the rooms occupied by the Royal Society of Arts.
5   What are the services of the Manpower Services Commission?
6   The Office of Fair Trading offers protection to the consumer.
7   Miss Jenkins moved from the Invoicing Department to Purchasing.

(43)

BUSINESS REPORTS

A business report may be a simple inter-office memorandum about the background of a would-be customer, or it may run into hundreds of pages and be as formal as a comparison of the relative merits of several proposed sites for a new factory, complete with facts and figures presented in tabular form. The formal report may be drafted and rewritten several times.

While an executive would prepare a report, it is usual for the typist to be responsible for the layout of the report and for the details of style.

Headings

Most formal business reports contain headings that introduce each main division or subdivision. When such headings are used, be consistent with display throughout the report.

Style

Consistency in style is also essential. For example, if at the beginning of a report business titles are typed in capitals, then they should not be typed in lower case later on.

Spacing

If you are typing a DRAFT, type this word at the top left margin of the first page and use double or treble spacing with wide margins $1\frac{1}{2}$" x 1". The final typing may be in double or single spacing.

Quotations

When preparing a business report, an executive may wish to quote excerpts from other sources. Brief quotations run in with text matter that introduces them, and are enclosed in quotation marks. Longer quotations should be started on a new line and preferably indented from the left margin. Quotation marks are typed at the beginning of each paragraph and at the end of the last paragraph.

SECTION D

Exercise 1   A4 paper.   Margins 20–85.   Single spacing.

P R O O F R E A D I N G

The most competent audio typist makes an error occasionally, but that error does not appear in the document placed on the employer's desk for signature. Because the audio typist has carefully proofread each page before it was taken from the machine, the error has been detected and it has been corrected.

IMPORTANCE

While proofreading has always been an essential part of the audio typist's training, it is now doubly important because if you wish to operate a word processing machine or an electronic typewriter, your ability to check quickly and correct errors in typing, spelling, grammar, etc, is even more meaningful.

ELECTRONIC MACHINES

Documents prepared on an electronic typewriter or a word processing machine are often used over and over again, and you can well imagine the disastrous results if you typed the wrong figures, were careless in checking your finished work, and your original error was then repeated hundreds of times.

Exercise 2   A5 portrait paper.   Margins 13–63.   Single spacing.

TRAVEL INFORMATION

HOTEL RESERVATIONS

Although you may be well informed about hotels and travel, you must be sure that the specific arrangements for a business trip are based on accurate, current information.

Booking Accommodation

It is usual to telephone and make a hotel reservation. Remember to specify the type of room required, the approximate price, the time of arrival, and the length of stay.

Written Confirmation

Immediately after making the hotel reservation, write a short letter confirming the booking. Where time permits, always ask the hotel for written confirmation, and, when writing to a hotel, address the letter to The Manager.

Unit 16

This unit consists of a passage dealing with the display of a business report, an annual report of a company, a letter and a memo from brief notes.

Job 1 (261 words)
A4 bond paper.
Double spacing and indented display.
Margins: 13–90
Main heading: BUSINESS REPORTS

Job 2
A4 bond paper.
Single spacing and blocked display.
Margins: 19–88
Copy from the handwritten exercise in your book.

Job 3 (118 words)
Letter.
A4 bond paper with a carbon copy on bank paper and an envelope.
Blocked display.
Margins: 19–88
From: F S Somers, 209 Bradford Street, Leeds, LS4 5SP
To: Union Insurance Co Ltd, Calvery Street, Leeds, LS1 3AE
Ref: FSS/IES   Date: Today's
Mark the letter and the envelope:
FOR THE ATTENTION OF THE MANAGER – CLAIMS DEPARTMENT
Heading: POLICY NO 1789

Job 4 (43 words)
Memo to be typed from brief notes.
A5 headed memo paper. Take one carbon copy.
Blocked display.
Margins: 13–90
From: J R Ingram, Sales Manager
To: Mrs F P Slater, Supply Department
Ref: JRI/OP   Date: 12 August 1985
Heading: TYPING: TWO-IN-ONE COURSE

Exercise 3   Type the following exercise on A5 landscape paper. Use side headings as in copy.

```
SPECIAL DAY EXCURSIONS

The West Midland Division

HASTINGS     Sunday 1 July.  From Wolverhampton, Birmingham New
             Street, and Coventry
             Adult: £7.00    Child: £3.50

BLACKPOOL    Tuesday 17 July.  From Coventry, Birmingham New
             Street, Dudley, and Wolverhampton
             Adult: £6.50    Child: £3.75

YORK         Wednesday 18 July.  From Banbury, Leamington Spa,
             Dorridge, and Solihull
             Adult: £6.30    Child: £3.10

NOTE: All the services will offer a Buffet Bar and the prices
will be: Tea £0.37, Coffee £0.50, Sandwiches £1.30, Biscuits £0.30
```

(Suggested tab stop and margins for the above exercise are given at the bottom of the next page.)

(19)
P O R K

The flesh of pork should be pale pink and finely grained, and the fat
firm and creamy white.

TIMETABLE FOR ROASTING PORK
(19)   (88)

Type of joint	(40) Roasting time at 220 °C (425 °F) Mark 7	(66) Roasting time at 190 °C (375 °F) Mark 5
Joints on the bone	25 minutes per 450 g (1 lb), plus 25 minutes	30–35 minutes per 450 g (1 lb), plus 25 minutes
Boned and rolled joints		30–35 minutes per 450 g (1 lb), plus 35 minutes

Orange Pork Chops (6 servings)

(50)

6 pork chops   225 ml (8 fl oz) orange juice
175 ml (6 fl oz) water   100 g (4 oz) sugar
2.5 ml (½ level tsp) paprika   15 ml (1 level tbsp) cornflour
1.25 ml (¼ level tsp) pepper   2.5 ml (½ level tsp) ground cinnamon
5 ml (1 level tsp) salt   12 whole cloves
1 orange

Method

1 Fry chops gently until well browned on both sides.

2 Add the water, pepper, 1 level tsp salt, and paprika and bring to the
   boil. Cover and simmer for about 35 minutes, turning once.

3 Put the orange rind and juice, cornflour, sugar and spices in a saucepan and cook and stir until thickened. Add the orange slices and
   remove from the heat.

4 Place the chops in a heated serving dish and pour the sauce and the
   orange slices over them.

Exercise 4　　　　　　A4 paper.　　Margins 20–85.　Double spacing.

REFERENCE BOOKS

Since much of the work of the audio typist consists of transcription, you will have frequent need to consult reference books for
verifying spelling, points of grammar, style, etc. The first
book on your list is, of course, the dictionary.

The Dictionary The modern dictionary is the most comprehensive
reference book ever published. Like any machine or tool, however,
the technique of using it correctly must be mastered if the greatest benefits are to be obtained.

Applied Typing The data bank section of this typing manual will
give you full information about typewriting conventions and acceptable methods of display.

Telephone Directories Directories in which you will find and verify telephone numbers. Invaluable for checking on spelling of
names and addresses. Yellow Pages aims to make it possible for
users to find quickly the goods and services they need.

Post Office Guide Published annually and gives information on
all departments of the Post Office, comprising principal services
and charges.

Exercise 3　　　　　　Tab stop at 20; margins 32–85.

PORK   ← sp caps

The flesh of pork shld be pale pink & finely grained, & the fat firm & creamy white.

TIMETABLE FOR ROASTING PORK

Type of joint	Roasting time at 220 °C (425 °F) Mark 7	Roasting time at 190 °C (375 °F) Mark 5
Joints on the bone	25 minutes per 450 g (1 lb), plus 25 mins	30-35 mins per 450 g (1 lb), plus 25 mins
Boned & rolled joints		30-35 mins per 450 g (1 lb), plus 35 mins

Orange Pork Chops   (6 servings)

6 pork chops
175 ml (6 fl oz) water
2.5 ml (½ level tsp) paprika
1.25 ml (¼ level tsp) pepper
5 ml (1 level tsp) salt
1 orange

225 ml (8 fl oz) orange juice
100 g (4 oz) sugar
15 ml (1 level tbsp) cornflour
2.5 ml (½ level tsp) ground cinnamon
12 whole cloves

Method

1 Fry chops gently until well browned on both sides.
2 Add the water, pepper, 1 level tsp salt, and paprika & bring to the boil. Cover & simmer f abt 35 mins, turning once.
3 Put the orange rind & juice, cornflour, sugar & spices in a saucepan & cook & stir until thickened. Add the orange slices & remove from the heat.
4 Place the chops in a heated serving dish & pour the sauce & orange slices over them.

Unit 5

This unit is divided into 4 sections.

SECTION A Eight numbered sentences containing homophones. Use A4 paper with margins of 13 and 90 and single spacing. Each sentence must by typed on a separate line, and you should listen to a complete sentence before starting to type. Before you finish typing a sentence, start to listen to the next one.

SECTION B In Section B, page 20, read the information dealing with the use of the apostrophe. In Section C you will be asked to type sentences based on the explanations and examples given.

SECTION C For both exercises use the same sheet of A4 paper and margins as for Section A.

Exercise 1 Eight numbered sentences incorporating the use of the apostrophe. Each sentence is to be typed on a separate line. Commas will not be dictated but should be inserted where appropriate.

Exercise 2 Seven numbered sentences incorporating the use of the apostrophe. Follow instructions given for Exercise 1.

SECTION D In this section there will be exercises with numbered or lettered items. Refer to page 43 of *TYPING: TWO-IN-ONE COURSE* if further guidance is required. Use blocked display and open punctuation.

You are reminded about developing your skill in displaying exercises. Look particularly at the number of words in an exercise and the amount of space it occupies when typed: note the difference between the space used in Job 1 (79 words and double spacing) and the space taken up by Job 3 (100 words and single spacing). Careful attention to this will mean that, later on, you will have little difficulty in deciding on paper size, margins, etc, when typing the assignments and when taking an audio transcription examination.

Job 1 (79 words) A5 landscape bond paper.
Information about layout of enumerated items. Type in double spacing. Margins 19–88.

Job 2 (35 words) A5 portrait bond paper.
A list of 7 items to be found in an office. Type in double spacing. Margins 13–64.

Job 3 (100 words) A5 portrait bond paper.
A list of dictating conventions that are used when dictating matter for audio transcription. Use single spacing. Margins 13–64.

A4 bond paper.   Double spacing.   Indented display.
Margins 19–88.

(50)
M E A T

Veal

Veal is a delicate meat with a subtle flavour and texture. Even though it is generally tender, it does require careful cooking to ensure that the quality and flavour are not lost. It should be cooked slowly to minimize the shrinkage and loss of moisture, but always cook very thoroughly as veal can be indigestible.

(Turn up 7 single spaces – 25 mm – for the timetable for roasting to be inserted.)

Lamb

The joints from young English lambs are small and expensive, but always tender. All cuts of lamb can be roasted (calculate the cooking time according to the timetable below), basting occasionally with the juices from the tin. Lamb is usually served medium to well done and the traditional accompaniment is mint sauce or redcurrant jelly.

(Turn up 7 single spaces – 25 mm – for the timetable for roasting to be inserted.)

Beef

The colour of good beef varies from bright red, when freshly cut, to a dark, brownish red after a few hours. Choose a cut suitable for the cooking method you intend to use. If roasting a very lean joint, add about 2 oz of cooking fat to the tin, and cook for the time given in the table below, basting with the juices from time to time.

(Make sure you have 25 mm clear for the timetable to be inserted, as well as a bottom margin of approximately 25 mm.)

Job 4 (80 words)   A5 landscape bond paper.
A list of some rules to be observed when dieting. Use double spacing. Any item that takes up more than one line should be typed in single spacing. Margins 19–88.

Job 3 A5 portrait bond paper. A5 bank paper.
Semi-blocked display. Margins 13–64.

(30)
46 Blossom Street
(29) Birmingham B21 6JU

4th January 1985

Dear Mr Greaves

I saw your advertisement in this week's edition
of the 'Home Advertiser', in which you state that you
are able to undertake decorating during the weekends
and evenings, at a much reduced cost.

Would you please arrange to call at my address
and let me have an estimate for decorating 2 bedrooms.
If you would be kind enough to telephone me on Monday
or Tuesday of next week, we can then arrange a convenient time for you to inspect the rooms.

My telephone number is 021-554 3021.

Yours sincerely

Suzanne Birchall (Mrs)

Mr T P Greaves
12 Ridgeway Road
BIRMINGHAM
B21 6RT

Job 2 A5 portrait bond paper. A5 bank paper. Blocked display.
Margins 13–64.

(33)
(22) 16 Westgate,
Mumbles, SWANSEA, Glam., SA5 2AA

2 June 1985

Dear Rev. Nicholson,

I was delighted to hear that the arrangements for
the Social Evening on Saturday, 14 July, have been
agreed by the Ladies' Committee.

There are a number of parishioners who will be
pleased to help; some to decorate the Church Hall,
others to prepare the buffet, and Mr. Stan Harris
has very kindly agreed to organize the sound effects,
microphone for speakers, etc.

I am making arrangements for the tombola. Hopefully,
we shall make a very good profit as so many people
have very generously donated the prizes, knowing that
the proceeds will go towards the Church roof.

Sincerely,

Rev. Michael Nicholson,
The Vicarage,
Mumbles,
SWANSEA,
Glam. SA5 3TA

SECTION A   A4 paper.   Margins 13–90.   Single spacing.   Use the same sheet for Exercises 1 and 2 in Section C.

```
1  The lecturer allowed us to leave at 6 in the afternoon.
2  The girl was rebuked for speaking aloud in the classroom.
3  Allow me to compliment you on the success of your dinner party.
4  The nuclear submarine had its full complement of officers and men.
5  If taxes are increased, I feel sure this will put a brake on inflation.
6  If you break that antique jug, you will most certainly have to pay for it.
7  It is essential that you purchase a television licence before next Tuesday.
8  Our firm has been licensed to sell tobacco, cigarettes, wines, and spirits.
```

SECTION B   In order to use the apostrophe correctly, you must have clear in your mind the difference between singular and plural nouns. For example: boy is singular, boys is plural. Man is singular, men is plural.
Compare these 2 sentences:
The boy's coat is in the hall.
(The coat belongs to the boy. The apostrophe before the s tells us that there is only one boy.)
The boys' coats are in the hall.
(The coats belong to the boys. The apostrophe after the s tells us that there is more than one boy.)

Use of the apostrophe to show possession

NUMBER 1   For a SINGULAR noun NOT ENDING IN s, add apostrophe s to the noun; for example:
(a) The audio typist's chair was very expensive.
     Our manager's desk needs replacing.
     The director's car is in the car park.
     Mary Brown's brief-case is in your office.
(b) The woman's records are in my filing cabinet.
     That man's golf bag had been lost.
     The child's toys had disappeared.

NUMBER 2   For a SINGULAR noun ENDING IN s, or an s sound, add apostrophe s to the noun; for example:
The headmistress's office was locked.
Mr James's suggestions were well received.

NUMBER 3   If the SINGULAR noun ENDS IN s, or an s sound, and the addition of an apostrophe s makes the word DIFFICULT TO PRONOUNCE, add the apostrophe only. What one considers DIFFICULT TO PRONOUNCE is debatable, and what is acceptable to one person may not be acceptable to another; the following examples could be argued about:
Mr John Bridges' son was captain of the cricket team.
Please ask Mr Jim Andrews' secretary to telephone me.
Have you read any of Charles Dickens' novels?

NUMBER 4   For a PLURAL noun ENDING IN s, add an apostrophe only; for example:
The audio typists' chairs were very expensive.
The directors' cars were in the car park.
(Compare these sentences with 1(a) above.)

NUMBER 5   For a PLURAL noun NOT ENDING IN s, add apostrophe s to the noun; for example:
The women's records are in my filing cabinet.
The men's golf bags had been lost.

(40)
FORMAT FOR PERSONAL LETTERS

I   PERSONAL BUSINESS LETTERS

These letters are used when writing to an unknown person or firm about a personal business matter. The layout is similar to that of a business letter. If your home address is not printed on your stationery, type it about 13 mm ($\frac{1}{2}$ in) from the top of the paper, and centre on the page, or type it so that the longest line ends flush with the right margin, all other lines starting at the same point. Date the letter in the usual place. The name and address of the addressee may be typed in the usual place or at the bottom left-hand margin, 2 spaces below your name.

II   FORMAL PERSONAL LETTERS

Formal personal letters are used when writing to someone older than yourself or to whom you owe respect. The layout is the same as for personal business letters; the salutation is formal, eg, Dear Ms Smith, Dear Mrs Taylor, Dear Dr Emery.

III   PERSONAL LETTERS

Used when writing to a personal friend. Your address and date are typed as in a personal business letter; no name and address of addressee; the salutation is informal, eg, Dear Mary, Dear Arthur, Dear Uncle George.

The children's toys had disappeared.
(You will notice that women, men, and children all end in en. Compare these sentences with 1(b) on page 20.)

NUMBER 6   For 2 or more nouns that show separate possession, add apostrophe s to all the nouns; for example:
This document requires the buyer's and the seller's signatures.
(Preferable to write: The buyer and the seller should sign the document.)

NUMBER 7   Apart from personal possessives (given above), apostrophes are required for impersonal possessives; for example:
Today's cricket match will start at 1000 hours.
I have just returned from 2 weeks' holiday.
The house was not a stone's throw away.

NUMBER 8   The apostrophe is NOT used in expressions such as:
The Matchmakers Association (Matchmakers does not have an apostrophe.)
The Sales Manager (Sales does not have an apostrophe).
Barclays Bank PLC (Barclays does not have an apostrophe.)

NUMBER 9   It would be unusual to insert the apostrophe in sentences such as:
The electronic typewriters function keys. It is better to say: The function keys of the electronic typewriter.
The roofs slates had been blown away. Better to say: The slates on the roof had been blown away.

NUMBER 10   The apostrophe is NOT used in the pronouns: hers, yours, ours, theirs and its. They are already possessive.

NUMBER 11   The apostrophe is NOT now used (to show omission) before words such as phone (telephone), bus (omnibus), plane (aeroplane); for example:
The phone number is 021–472 2677.
The bus leaves the depot at 9 o'clock in the morning.

Use of the apostrophe to show omission of letters

NUMBER 12   The apostrophe is also used to show the OMISSION OF LETTERS in words – known as elision; for example:
I don't know what time the train arrives.
I'm glad that you are calling tomorrow.
We'd like to show you our landscaped garden.
It's time to say goodbye.
(Notice the difference between IT'S (which means it is) and the pronoun ITS as used in the following sentence: The dog chased its tail.)

NOTE In typewritten documents, do not use elision unless you are quoting direct speech, or unless you have been given instructions to do so.

NUMBER 13   To avoid confusing the reader, use the apostrophe in the following and similar expressions:
Mind your p's and q's.
The word accommodation has 2 c's and 2 m's.

NUMBER 14   DO NOT use the apostrophe for the PLURAL of ABBREVIATIONS and PLURAL of FIGURES; for example:
Two MPs are to give the lectures.
I think he died in the early 1950s.

NUMBER 15   The apostrophe is used to represent FEET and MINUTES; for example:
The door measured 6′ 9″ × 3′ 6″.
One degree equals 60′, and 1′ equals 60″.

Unit 15

This unit contains personal letters and display exercises with space left for diagrams, etc.

Job 1 (203 words)
A4 bond paper.
Passage giving the format for personal letters.
Use the indented form of display.
Double spacing. Margins: 19–88.
Heading: FORMAT FOR PERSONAL LETTERS

Job 2 (102 words)
Letter on A5 portrait bond paper with carbon copy on bank paper.
From: 16 Westgate, Mumbles, Swansea, Glam., SA5 2AA
To: Rev. Michael Nicholson, The Vicarage, Mumbles, Swansea, Glam., SA5 3TA, to be inserted after complimentary close.
Date: 2 June 1985   Margins: 13–64
Blocked display and full punctuation.
Type an envelope.

Job 3 (94 words)
Letter on A5 portrait bond paper with carbon copy on bank paper.
From: Mrs Suzanne Birchall, 46 Blossom Street, Birmingham, B21 6JU
To: Mr T P Greaves, 12 Ridgeway Road, Birmingham, B21 6RT
Date: 4th January 1985   Margins: 13–64
Semi-blocked display and open punctuation.
Type an envelope.

Job 4 (182 words)
A4 bond paper. Double spacing. Indented display.
An article in double spacing about 3 different types of meat. It will be necessary to leave spaces for information to be inserted at a later date.
Main heading: MEAT   Margins: 19–88

Job 5
An article about pork to be typed from the handwritten draft in your book.

SECTION C

Exercise 1   Same paper and margins as used for Section A.

    1 We thought it was no business of ours.
    2 The shop window was full of children's toys.
    3 The men's hairdressing salon is closed on Thursdays.
    4 The Sales Manager's Conference was held in Blackpool.
    5 Mrs Jones's silver wedding is next Saturday, 21 December.
    6 Evidence was given that there were 2 PCs in the police car.
    7 The ladies' golf tournament is on Monday, 15 September 1985.
    8 A year's dividend is now due on the preference shares that I hold.

Exercise 2

    1 You will receive a gift of 12 months' subscription to the magazine.
    2 Today's computers embody the latest developments in high technology.
    3 Despite the weather, the stockholders' meeting was very well attended.
    4 Britain's EEC ministers will discuss the financial contribution today.
    5 The British Travel Agents Association will forward all details to you.
    6 The Directors' meetings were held yesterday afternoon in the boardroom.
    7 The Managing Director's secretary, Beryl Smith, is on holiday this week.

SECTION D

Job 1   A5 landscape bond paper.   Margins 19–88.   Double spacing.

NUMBERED OR LETTERED PARAGRAPHS OR ITEMS

Paragraphs or items may be numbered or lettered so that the reader

may more easily understand the content. This is called enumeration.

The numbers or letters may stand on their own or be enclosed in

brackets. It is usual to leave 2 spaces after the last figure,

letter or bracket. Turn to page 43 in Typing: Two-in-One Course

to see how the exercises with enumerated items are displayed before

typing the next Jobs on the tape.

Job 3 (continued)

Messrs. Bayliss & Henderson   2   Today's date

are fully furnished and serviced, and are within easy reach of the
main tourist attractions, shops, restaurants, etc. The surrounding
countryside has a wealth of beautiful scenery.

    Should you require more information on any of these properties,
please contact me again.

                      Yours faithfully,

                      James Hamilton

Enc.

Job 4   A4 headed paper.   Semi-blocked display.   Margins 19–88.

Ref. AFW/BC   Date as postmark

Dear Member,

    From your Membership Card, which gives details of this session's
events, you will see that our next meeting is a visit to the theatre
on 7 January to see the opening performance of the play 'Chase Me
Comrade'. Tickets are £2.50 each, and the play begins at 8.00 p.m.

    If you wish me to reserve any tickets for you, will you please
fill in the form below and return to me not later than Friday,
20 December, together with a remittance.

                      Yours sincerely,

                      Andrew F. Williams

                      Social Secretary

Andrew F. Williams, Social Secretary, Dossett & Parnell (International)
Ltd., 26 High Street, Highbury, London, N5 1UD.

    Please reserve .... seats for the Theatre visit on

7 January, for which I enclose Cheque/Postal Order for ....

Name ....

Address ....

    ....

Job 2   A5 portrait bond paper.   Margins 13–64.   Double spacing.

ITEMS TO BE FOUND IN AN OFFICE

The following essential items will be found in most offices:

1 Telephone

2 Stapling machine

3 Duplicator

4 Typewriter

5 Two-hole punch

6 Filing cabinet

7 Photo-copying machine.

Job 3   A5 portrait bond paper.   Margins 13–64.   Single spacing.

AUDIO TRANSCRIPTION

<u>Some Dictating Conventions</u>

The following points should be noted before commencing your audio transcription course.

(a) New paragraphs will be indicated.

(b) All punctuation marks (with the exception of the comma and apostrophe) will be dictated.

(c) The spelling of unusual words will be given after the word has been dictated. The Post Office phonetic alphabet will be used only when dictating single letters which need identification.

(d) If a word is to be underscored, the instruction 'underscore' will be given after the word has been dictated.

(e) Any specific instructions for headings will precede the words of the heading.

A4 headed paper.   A4 plain bond paper.   A4 bank paper.
Semi-blocked display.   Margins 19–88.

Our ref. VS/Prop/4847   Today's date

Your ref. JR/Lettings

FOR THE ATTENTION OF MISS T. J. GITTINS

Messrs. Bayliss & Henderson,
Chartered Surveyors and Property Consultants,
30 Brandhall Avenue,
TORQUAY,
Devon.
TQ2 1AA

Dear Sirs,
                        (38)
                LETTING/ADMINISTRATION SERVICE

     Our Administration Service is run primarily for owners who wish
to let their property to family/friends only, as arranged by themselves
or with the assistance of our Letting Service. This Administration
Service involves regular inspections of properties to check for such
things as water leakage or other damage, etc. These inspections are
usually made after heavy rainfall, as an extra precaution. Prior to
the arrival of the owner or tenant, the premises are checked for clean-
liness and cleaned if necessary. The water supply, gas, and electricty
are also checked. On departure, cleaning and laundry are arranged.

     Owners are advised to insure property. This covers them against
damage which might be caused to their property. Insurance can be
arranged, at reasonable rates, with any well-known insurance company.

     The Letting Service includes:

     (a)   attention to the tenants arranged by the owners; and/or

     (b)   letting the property for owners.

HOUSES AND FLATS TO RENT

     As part of our Letting/Administration Service to owners of property,
we can offer, on their behalf, a wide range of houses/flats to rent
throughout the year. We anticipate these are for people who prefer to
organize their own holiday, etc. - to go by car, or make their own travel
arrangements.

     These properties are offered at reasonable rentals, and the enclosed
list covers a wide range of properties presently available. All properties

---

D I E T I N G

It is always difficult to lose weight, but the following rules should

be observed when trying to keep to a diet.

A   Do not eat more than 4 oz of butter a week.

B   Do not drink more than half a pint of milk per day.

C   Do not eat more than 5 oz of bread per day.

D   Do not eat any fatty foods, fried foods, sweets, sugar, cream, cakes,
biscuits or nuts, and drink only unsweetened tea, coffee or squashes.

A4 headed paper.   A4 bank paper.   Semi-blocked display.
Margins 19–88.

Our ref ACM/4/312   Today's date

FOR THE ATTENTION OF THE OFFICE MANAGER

L F Davis & Co Ltd
Eden Vale
WEYBRIDGE
Surrey
KT15 2AA

Dear Sirs
                               (45)
                          OFFICE FURNITURE

     The enclosed catalogue has been specially compiled to assist
our customers in making their selection of wooden and metal office
furniture. Space does not permit us to illustrate all the items in
our large and varied range, and we, therefore, suggest that you com-
municate with us if you are unable to find, in the catalogue, the
particular article you are seeking.

     We would like to draw your special attention to the following
second-hand cabinets, illustrations of which will be found on page 30
of the catalogue:

(31)		Heavy duty steel cabinets, in 4-drawer units	
(44)		Excellent condition	
		(41)	(67)
(34)	SC64	5' 0" wide x 3' 6" high	£30.00
(34)	SC65	6' 6" wide x 4' 6" high	£32.50
(34)	SC66	8' 0" wide x 5' 6" high	£40.75

     If you are interested in these particular cabinets, we recommend
you to send us your order without delay, as there are only a few
available.

                          (53) Yours faithfully
                          (53) DOSSETT & PARNELL (INTERNATIONAL) LTD

     Enc

Unit 6

This unit is divided into 4 sections.

SECTION A   Eight numbered sentences containing words that may be difficult to spell. Use A4 paper and margins of 13 and 90. You must type each sentence on a separate line, and you should listen to a complete sentence before starting to type. Before you finish typing a sentence, start listening to the next one.

SECTION B   In Section B, page 27, read the information dealing with the use of the full stop, question mark and exclamation mark. In Section C you will be asked to type sentences based on the explanations and examples given.

SECTION C   Exercises covering words and points introduced in Units 1–6.

Exercise 1 (84 words)   A5 portrait paper and single spacing. Main heading, subheading, paragraph heading. Margins 13–63.

Exercise 2 (100 words)   A4 paper and double spacing. Main heading, subheading, paragraph heading. Margins 20–85.

Exercise 3 (80 words)   A5 landscape paper and single spacing. Main heading. Margins 20–85.

Exercise 4 (103 words)   A4 paper and double spacing. Main heading, subheading, shoulder headings. Margins 20–85.

Exercise 5 (110 words)   A4 paper and single spacing. Main heading, subheading and side headings. Set tab stop at 19; left margin 35; right margin 88.

You are reminded about developing your skill in displaying exercises. Note particularly the extra space taken up by double spacing, headings and enumerated items.

SECTION D   A5 memoranda. Use blocked display and open punctuation. Headed memo paper may be duplicated from the copy given in *AUDIO TRANSCRIPTION, TEACHER'S MANUAL.* Margins 13–90.

Job 1 (105 words)   Type on A5 headed memo paper.
From: Social Work Adviser
To: Area Director   Date: 17 July 1985
Heading: MRS IVY PRINGLE, 16 PARK ROAD, DEVONPORT
Ref: 2094/IP/NP/RM

Job 2 (103 words)   Type on A5 headed memo paper. It contains enumerated items.
From: Harry J Foley, Area Director
To: N Patel, Social Work Adviser
Heading: As in Job 1
Ref: 2094/IP/HF/JS   Date: 19 July 1985
The following names and addresses will be dictated:
Mr Norman Austin, 58 Highfield Road
Mr Sidney Carran, 22 Porchester Drive
Mrs Doris Heard, 18 Trinity Flats
Miss Molly Milford, 68 Station Road

Job 1   A4 headed paper.   A4 bank paper.   Semi-blocked display.
Margins 19–88.

Your ref. ORD.3118   Today's date

Our ref. AT/gg

FOR THE ATTENTION OF THE PRODUCTION MANAGER

Messrs. F. J. Lowe & Son,
20 Westgate Street,
CARDIFF.
CF4 2BT

Dear Sirs,
                            (45)
                     ORDER NUMBER 3118

      In sending you our confirmation of order, for which we thank
you, we would point out that to facilitate matters we have, in this
instance, accepted the order on the terms applied to you in the first
6 months of the past year. Unfortunately, however, the rising costs
of production and, in particular, the considerable increases in wages
due to the award made to workers, force us to revise our prices for
future orders.

      Before sending further orders, which we hope we shall still be
receiving from you, we must request you to ask us to quote you our
up-to-date prices. When doing so, we shall always take into consideration our good relations, and, especially, the quantity of appliances
which you intend to order.

      To suit your convenience, we can accept an order for a larger
quantity to be executed by deliveries spread over a certain period,
e.g., every 3 or 4 months. This larger quantity would enable you to
have the benefit of more favourable prices.
                            (53)
                     Yours faithfully,
                     DOSSETT & PARNELL (INTERNATIONAL) LTD.

                     Sales Department

Job 3 (139 words)	Type on A5 headed memo paper with carbon copy on bank paper.
	From: James Dale, General Manger
	To: Mr Clive Smith, Bookings Manager
	Heading: SMYTHE-PARKER'S WEDDING TRANSPORT
	Ref: JD/A10 Today's date

Job 4 (84 words)

Memo on A5 headed paper with carbon copy on bank paper.
From: Personnel Manger
To: All Staff
Heading: TEA BREAKS
Ref: PM/WR/HI   Today's date

Job 5 (91 words)

Type on A5 headed memo paper with carbon copy on bank paper.
From: Miss F R McDowell, Office Superintendent
To: Section Officers
Heading: ANNUAL OUTING
Ref: FRMc/TRH   Today's date

Job 6 (95 words)

Type on A5 headed memo paper with carbon copy on bank paper.
From: Product Manger, Vocational Education
To: Mr A Drummond
Heading: TYPING: TWO-IN-ONE COURSE
Ref: TG/McGH/OP   Today's date

Job 7 (90 words)

A4 bond paper.
Type from manuscript copy the enclosure to be attached to the memo in Job 6.

Job 4 (122 words)

Circular letter on A4 headed paper.
(Headed paper may be used from *AUDIO TRANSCRIPTION, TEACHER'S MANUAL.*)
From: Andrew F. Williams, Social Secretary, Dossett & Parnell (International) Ltd., 26 High Street, Highbury, London, N5 1UD.
Date as postmark   Margins: 19–88 Ref.: AFW/BC
Use the semi-blocked style of display and full punctuation.
Type the tear-off portion at the foot of the letter in double spacing.

SECTION A   A4 paper.   Margins 13–90.   Single spacing.

1 They preferred not to press charges.
2 The committee will meet at 2.30 pm today.
3 It is a privilege to meet such a brave person.
4 I was exhausted at the end of the sales conference.
5 The hockey match on Tuesday will be a special occasion.
6 The sailors guarded the entrance to the naval dockyard.
7 The staff were terrified by the sudden appearance of a masked man.
8 It will be unnecessary to transfer your bank account to another branch.

SECTION B   Today I am going to remind you about when to use the full stop, the question mark and the exclamation mark.

The full stop is used

NUMBER 1   At the end of a complete sentence; for example:
The Financial Director, Mr L Arrowsmith, was not at the meeting.
Tell the Company Secretary that I will be late.

NOTE   If the sentence ends with a question mark or exclamation mark, no additional full stop is required, nor should an extra full stop be typed if the sentence ends with an abbreviation which already has a full stop.

NUMBER 2   To indicate omission of words from quoted matter, 3 spaced full stops are used; for example:
'. . . omission of words from quoted matter, 3 spaced full stops are used.'

NUMBER 3   As a decimal point typed on the line; for example:
The sheet measures $1.20 \times 5.81 \times 2.54$ m.
You will notice that there is a space before and after the small x for the multiply sign.

NUMBER 4   Within decimal enumeration; for example:
4.1 In decimal enumeration, use the decimal point, followed by a figure, for the subdivision.

NUMBER 5   With full punctuation in enumerated items, after the number of the item (arabic figures or roman numerals); for example:
5. With full punctuation, etc.

NUMBER 6   To separate hours from minutes in expressing time; for example:
The conference will open at 6.30 pm. (open punctuation)
The conference will open at 6.30 p.m. (full punctuation)

NOTE   (a) The full stop must be inserted between hours and minutes, even with open punctuation.
(b) Figures are always used with am and pm.
(c) There is no full stop in the 24-hour clock, even with full punctuation; for example: My train will leave at 1830 hours.
(d) The 24-hour clock starts at 0001 and ends at 2359. For 2400 hours type midnight and the date; for example: The cruise starts at midnight on 23 June.

Unit 14

This unit consists of semi-blocked letters. Follow the instructions carefully.

Job 1 (182 words) Letter on A4 headed paper with a carbon copy on bank paper.
(Headed paper may be used from *AUDIO TRANSCRIPTION, TEACHER'S MANUAL.*)
From: Dossett & Parnell (International) Ltd., 26 High Street, Highbury, London, N5 1UD.
To: Messrs. F. J. Lowe & Son, 20 Westgate Street, Cardiff, CF4 2BT.
Mark the letter FOR THE ATTENTION OF THE PRODUCTION MANAGER
Your ref.: ORD.3118   Our ref.: AT/gg   Date: Today's
Heading: ORDER NUMBER 3118   Margins: 19–88
Use the semi-blocked style of display and full punctuation.
Type an envelope.

Job 2 (161 words) Letter on A4 headed paper with a carbon copy on bank paper and an envelope.
(Headed paper may be used from *AUDIO TRANSCRIPTION, TEACHER'S MANUAL.*)
From: Dossett & Parnell (International) Ltd, 26 High Street, Highbury, London, N5 1UD
To: L F Davis & Co Ltd, Eden Vale, Weybridge, Surrey, KT15 2AA
Mark the letter FOR THE ATTENTION OF THE OFFICE MANAGER
Our ref: ACM/4/312   Date: Today's   Margins: 19–88
Heading: OFFICE FURNITURE
The following information is to be incorporated in the letter:
Heavy duty steel cabinets, in 4-drawer units
Excellent condition

SC64   5′ 0″ wide x 3′ 6″ high £30.00

SC65   6′ 6″ wide x 4′ 6″ high £32.50

SC66   8′ 0″ wide x 5′ 6″ high £40.75
Use the semi-blocked style of display and open punctuation.

Job 3 (295 words) Letter on A4 headed paper with a continuation sheet and a carbon copy on bank paper.
(Headed paper may be used from *AUDIO TRANSCRIPTION, TEACHER'S MANUAL.*)
From: Dossett & Parnell (International) Ltd., 26 High Street, Highbury, London, N5 1UD.
To: Messrs. Bayliss & Henderson, Chartered Surveyors and Property Consultants, 30 Brandhall Avenue, Torquay, Devon, TQ2 1AA.
Mark the letter FOR THE ATTENTION OF MISS T. J. GITTINS
Our ref.: VS/Prop/4847   Your ref.: JR/Lettings   Date: Today's
Heading: LETTING/ADMINISTRATION SERVICE   Margins: 19–88
Use the semi-blocked style of display and full punctuation.
Type an envelope.

NUMBER 7   After initials and abbreviations with full punctuation; for example:

J. H. Black & Co. Ltd.

Mrs. R. Bates, M.A., B.Sc.

NOTE (a) Certain abbreviations and acronyms may be typed without full stops even when using full punctuation. Here are a few examples: VAT, NATO, PAYE, UK, USA, RSA, LCCI, BBC.

(b) Full stops are never inserted in abbreviations used for metric measurements.

(c) Full stops must be inserted with imperial measurements when using full punctuation.

The question mark is used

NUMBER 8   To end a sentence that asks a question; for example:

When are you leaving for Australia?

Where is the cheque from K L David & Company?

NOTE (a) Do not use a question mark for a polite request; for example: Will you please let me know when the goods arrive.

(b) There is no space before a question mark at the end of a sentence, but there are 2 spaces after it.

NUMBER 9   To express doubt or uncertainty, and, when used in this way, it should be enclosed in brackets; for example:

His explanation (?) was supposed to be a plausible one.

NOTE Normally one would avoid such usage in business correspondence.

The exclamation mark is used

NUMBER 10   To end a sentence or expression showing strong emotion, surprise, feeling, etc; for example:

Congratulations!   I hope you will be very happy.

Before crossing the road: Stop!   Look!   Listen!

NOTE (a) The exclamation mark should be used sparingly; otherwise, it loses its value.

(b) Most electronic typewriters have an exclamation mark key. If your typewriter does not, type an apostrophe, backspace and type a full stop.

(c) There is no space between the last letter and the exclamation mark at the end of a sentence, but there are 2 spaces after it.

SECTION C

Exercise 1   A5 portrait paper.   Margins 13–63. ·   Single spacing.

```
R G WILLIAMS & CO LTD

Electronic Typewriter Excelsior 103

STATIONERY ORDER 09/85  I feel it is important that
you fulfil the promise you made about the delivery
of the magnetic recording floppy diskettes to the
above company.

It has just occurred to me that I will be leaving
for Inverness next Tuesday, and I could easily
deliver the diskettes and the stationery while I
am there.  Therefore, would you please arrange for
our warehouse to have the goods ready by 5 pm on
Monday evening.
```

A4 bond paper.   Double spacing.

(29)
BUDGET FOR THE YEAR ENDED 31 DECEMBER 1984

(20)   (80)

Items	Net exclusive of VAT	VAT	Total inclusive of VAT
	£	£	£
(22) Annual Outing	247.00	37.05	284.05
Insurance	5.50	Exempt	5.50
Meeting Expenses	204.94	30.74	235.68
Postage	194.14	Exempt	194.14
Printing and Stationery	139.63	20.94	160.57
Telephone and Telex ...	147.69	22.15	169.84
Travelling Expenses			
Train Fares	194.00	Zero Rated	194.00
TOTAL	£1,132.90	£110.88	£1,243.78

1st tab: 48; 2nd tab: 60; 3rd tab 70

Exercise 2   A4 paper.   Double spacing.   Margins used 20–85.

B R I G H T O N   T E N N I S   T O U R N A M E N T

24-29 JUNE 1985

Hotel Accommodation Mrs Thatcher, whom you spoke to yesterday,

was privileged to receive an invitation to the tennis match, and

she will need the following accommodation: single room with

shower, sea view, TV, and telephone. From the subheading above,

you will see that she requires the accommodation from 24-29 June,

ie, from the evening of 24 June to the morning of 29 June.

Having completed her long and detailed report on the IMPORTANCE

OF EXPORTS, she is entitled to a holiday. If you would book the

accommodation, I should be grateful.

Exercise 3   A5 landscape paper.   Single spacing.   Margins used 20–85.

MARGARET

C O N G R A T U L A T I O N S !

I was delighted to hear that you passed your final examination.
Will you now take your 2 weeks' holiday? If you have time to
spare, I could use a competent typist for 2 or 3 days. I have
2 committee meetings next Tuesday and should be glad if you would
type the Minutes for me.

Wednesday is a special occasion as it is Jean's twenty-first
birthday, and celebrations will start at 7.30 for 8.00 pm in the
Students Union Hall.

Job 5　　　　　　A5 headed memo paper.　　A5 bank paper.　　Indented display.
　　　　　　　　　　Margins 13–90.

M E M O R A N D U M

FROM　Winifred F. Salmons　　　　　　　　　　　　REF.　WFS/uy

TO　　Ms. J. P. Arrowsmith　　　　　　　　　　　　DATE　24 January 1985
　　　　(30)
　　　　BUDGET FOR THE YEAR ENDED 31 DECEMBER 1984

　　I am attaching a copy of our Budget for the year ended in December 1984.

　　Please let me have your comments on this as soon as possible, as I have
to report to the Board in 2 weeks' time.

Att.

Job 6　　　　　　　　A4 bond paper.　　　Double spacing.

Budget for the year ended 31 Dec '84 ← u.c. & u/score

Items	Net exclusive of VAT	VAT	Total inclusive of VAT	
	£	£	£	
Annual Outing	247.00	37.05	284.05	
Insurance . . .	5.50	Exempt	5.50	
Meeting Expenses . . .	204.94	30.74	235.68	
Postage	194.14	Exempt	194.14	
Printing & Stationery	147.69	22.15	169.84	Trs
Telephone & Telex . .	139.63	20.94	160.57	
Travelling Expenses		Zero		
Train Fares	194.00	Rated	194.00	
TOTAL . . .	£1,132;90	£110.88	£1,234,78	

HOME IMPROVEMENTS

Outstanding Craftsmen

DOUBLE GLAZING

Maintenance-free replacement aluminium windows and doors -

within our range there is a style just right for your home.

WORKMANSHIP

All our products are made on our own premises using top-quality

material. We will be pleased to arrange a visit to our factory

and showroom so that you can see for yourself the care and atten-

tion given to each and every order.

INSTALLATIONS

All installations are made by our own fitters who will carry out

your home improvements carefully, speedily, and efficiently.

Job 3 (continued)

Managing Director   2   3 June 1985

SALES PAMPHLETS

It was generally felt that the black-and-white pamphlets could be made much more attractive if colours were used. The Sales Manager agreed to look into costs and report to the Board.

ANNUAL HOLIDAYS

Dates for annual holidays to be sent to the Sales Director by 31 May, but representatives should note that Sales Promotion Week takes place from 2-6 September, and should therefore avoid booking holidays at this time.

I am enclosing a draft giving the outline of the programme for Sales Promotion Week.

Enc.

Job 4   A5 headed memo paper.   A5 bank paper.   Indented display.
                                       Margins 13–90.

M E M O R A N D U M

FROM   D. W. Bennett   REF.   DWB/BR

TO   Mr. J. Cornhill   DATE   Today's
                                       (45)
                                 ADVERTISEMENT

The Board has suggested that the following advertisement should be inserted in the 'Evening Mail' next month.

(40)   CLEAN-CAR SERVICES LTD.
(34)   Trafalgar Street, Burnley, BB11 1LJ

(39)   specialize in providing a
(42)   RAPID and EFFICIENT
(43)   car-wash service

(39)   Book of 20 Vouchers – £15
(36)   (Valid Monday to Thursday only)

(31)   OPEN: 8 a.m. – 6 p.m. Monday to Saturday

Exercise 5 A4 paper. Side headings. Single spacing. Margins 35–88.
Tab stop 19.

PERSONAL STATIONERY

<u>All Top-quality Paper</u>

LAYOUT STYLES   Choose either the space-saving style or the centred
                style.

PRICES   See our price-list for most of our standard lines.

COLOURED INKS   Our price-list provides for printing in BLACK or BLUE
                ink. Other colours can be supplied subject to a small
                additional charge.

ORDERING   It helps us to make sure we give you what you want if
                you use one of our order forms, but if you do not
                have an order form, simply put your requirements down
                on paper.

DELIVERY   At most times of the year we aim to despatch stationery
                orders within 14 working days.

A4 headed memo paper.   A4 bond paper.   A4 bank paper.
Indented display.   Margins 13–90.

M E M O R A N D U M

FROM   Sales Manager   REF.   PRT/SMan/250/JMB

TO   Managing Director   DATE   3 June 1985
                        (38)
                        SALES MEETING – 22 MAY 1985

For your information, I have set out below a summary of the discussion which took place at the meeting held on 22 May.

CALLS

It was agreed that all representatives must decide for themselves the amount of time spent with a customer. However, it was emphasized by the Sales Manager that time must not be wasted!

EXPENSES

The Board of Directors were concerned over the very high entertainment expenses incurred during the past 6 months. While it was agreed that, in order to keep the goodwill of certain clients, some expenses must obviously be incurred, it was necessary for this expenditure to be kept down to a minimum.

Representatives were asked to submit reasons for all entertainment expenses amounting to more than £10 in any one instance.

DAILY REPORTS

All representatives were supplied with mini portable recorders and were asked to record the result of an interview immediately after the interview, and post the information to their Branch Office each afternoon, so that the typists could transcribe these first thing each morning.

ORDERS

All orders received must be written on the official pads and 2 copies sent to Branch Offices immediately.

Where orders were urgent, these could be placed by telephone, but written confirmation must be sent by post.

ADVERTISING

Several representatives said they felt that more use could be made of advertising in local newspapers. The Sales Manager agreed to discuss this with the Board.

/continued

SECTION D

Job 1   A5 headed memo paper.   Single spacing.   Margins 13–90.

M E M O R A N D U M

From   Social Work Adviser

To   Area Director

Date   17 July 1985

MRS IVY PRINGLE, 16 PARK ROAD, DEVONPORT

The above-named lady, who is 82 years of age, is living alone in her own house.
Until quite recently she has coped very well with the aid of a home help, and
her daughter visiting her twice a week.

Recently, however, neighbours have complained that she has been wandering outside, and her doctor reports that she has become ill.

I would like to refer her for day care at the Laurels Centre. She will require
transport, and I would like you to visit her. I recommend she attends for the
full 5 days, if possible, and has a lunch every day.

2094/IP/NP/RM

Job 2   A5 headed memo paper.   Single spacing.   Margins 13–90.

M E M O R A N D U M

From   Harry J Foley, Area Director

To   N Patel, Social Work Adviser

Date   19 July 1985

MRS IVY PRINGLE, 16 PARK ROAD, DEVONPORT

Thank you for your memo dated 17 July regarding Mrs Ivy Pringle.

I understand your request for Mrs Pringle to be assessed for day care at the
Laurels, following a recommendation from her daughter and her GP. I must point
out, however, that we do have a waiting list, and the following persons are
high priority on that list.

1 Mr Norman Austin, 58 Highfield Road
2 Mr Sidney Carran, 22 Porchester Drive
3 Mrs Doris Heard, 18 Trinity Flats
4 Miss Molly Milford, 68 Station Road

I am enclosing the Minutes of the meeting, held last month, which give the
background notes on the above cases.

2094/IP/HF/JS

Enc

(35)   C O N T I N U A T I O N   S H E E T S

(43) Letters and Memoranda

A long letter or memo may require a second sheet. This is called a continuation sheet, and sometimes the name or initials of the sender are printed in the top left corner. Otherwise, always use a plain sheet the same size, colour, and quality as the letterhead.

The following details should be typed at the top of the second and subsequent pages: name of addressee, page number and date, starting on the fourth single line from the top. In fully-blocked letters or memos, all these details are typed at the left margin in double spacing in the following order: page number, date, name of addressee. In indented letters or memos, the name of the addressee is typed at the left margin, the page number is centred in the typing line, and the date ends at the right margin (from right margin backspace one for one to find starting point). The letter or memo is continued on the third single space below the continuation sheet details.

When a continuation sheet is needed, the letter or memo must be so arranged that at least 3 or 4 lines are carried to the second page. Do not divide a word from one page to the next.

The word 'continued', or 'PTO', may be used. A catchword, i.e., the first word appearing on the continuation page, is sometimes used.

Job 3   A5 headed memo paper.   Single spacing.   Margins 13–90.

M E M O R A N D U M

From   James Dale, General Manager

To   Mr Clive Smith, Bookings Manager

Date   Today's

SMYTHE-PARKER'S WEDDING TRANSPORT

I understand that our Company is handling all the transport arrangements for this important wedding. I hope all the details have been finalized, because you will be aware that Mr Norman Smythe-Parker, the bride's father, is our local Member of Parliament.

There is one important additional arrangement I would like you to make. I have just heard that the Mayor's car is 'off the road', and I would like you to ensure that the Mayor and Mayoress are collected from their home and taken to the church to arrive not later than 1145 hours.

Will you please ensure that 2 copies of the enclosed Order of Service are given to the Mayor and Mayoress as soon as they are collected.

JD/A10

Enc

Job 4   A5 headed memo paper.   Single spacing.   Margins 13–90.

M E M O R A N D U M

From   Personnel Manager

To   All Staff

Date   Today's

TEA BREAKS

My attention has been drawn to the fact that staff in Sections B and C are taking longer than the prescribed quarter of an hour for the afternoon tea break.

Will all staff kindly ensure that, from now on, tea breaks do not exceed the prescribed time, ie, 1530-1545.

This memo applies equally to those who use the staff canteen as well as to those who remain in their sections and make their own tea.

PM/WR/HI

(31)
OPEN AND FULL PUNCTUATION, AND ABBREVIATIONS

You are using indented paragraphs and centring the main heading
to this exercise. Refer to Typing: Two-in-One Course pages 86 and
89 if you are unsure of the correct procedure to adopt.

Open Punctuation

Up to this point in the course all the exercises have been displayed with open punctuation. This means that full stops have not
been inserted after abbreviations, and letters have been typed with
the omission of commas after each line of the address, and after the
salutation and complimentary close. The modern trend is to omit
punctuation in those cases as it simplifies and speeds up the work
of the typist. However, punctuation is always inserted in sentences,
so that the grammatical sense is clear.

Full Punctuation

It is also acceptable to insert punctuation after abbreviations
and after each line of an address in a letter, as well as after the
salutation and complimentary close. Grammatical punctuation is always
inserted. Open and full punctuation must NEVER be mixed; a document
must be typed in either open or full punctuation.

Abbreviations

In typewritten work abbreviations should not, as a rule, be used.
There are, however, a few standard abbreviations which are never typed
in full and others which may be used in certain circumstances. Study
the lists on pages 84 and 85 in Typing: Two-in-One-Course, so that you
will know when not to use abbreviations and when it is permissible to
use them. You must always be consistent in their use, as well as the
use of either open or full punctuation.

Job 5   A5 headed memo paper.   Single spacing.   Margins 13–90.

M E M O R A N D U M

From Miss F R McDowell, Office Superintendent

To   Section Officers

Date Today's

ANNUAL OUTING

I enclose details of the annual outing which is to be held in 4 weeks' time
in London.

Please ensure that all staff are made aware of this information, and that
names of all those wishing to attend are handed to Mrs Sugar not later than
a week on Monday.

Will members of staff please indicate which of the following 2 theatres they
would prefer to visit.

(a) The Boy Friend, The Old Vic.

(b) Singin' in the Rain, The London Palladium.

FRMc/TRH

Enc

Job 6   A5 headed memo paper.   Single spacing.   Margins 13–90.

M E M O R A N D U M

From Product Manager, Vocational Education

To Mr A Drummond

Date Today's

TYPING: TWO-IN-ONE COURSE

I am enclosing a sample package of the promotion mailed to Colleges of Further
Education and to Secondary Schools for distribution to staff.

The information is sent, in the first place, to the Librarian who, it is hoped,
will distribute it to the teaching staff concerned.

We wish to include a poster advertising Typing: Two-in-One Course. Do you
feel the enclosed draft would be suitable for the front cover?

I should be very glad to have your comments as soon as possible.

TG/McGH/OP

Encs

Job 6

This is the enclosure to the previous memo and is a table showing the budget for the year ended 31 December 1984.
A4 bond paper. Double spacing.
Rule in ink or by means of the underscore. Check the totals.

Display the following exercise on a sheet of A4 bond paper.

TAKE A NEW AND FRESH APPROACH WITH

TYPING: TWO-IN-ONE COURSE ← — u/score

Archie Drummond
Anne Coles-Mogford
with Ida Scattergood

One Course – Two levels of Achievement

*   Clear & positive instructions

*   Well-planned, making use of time available

*   Full coverage of intermediate requirements

All the the factors of a changing market & environment are taken into a/c in this new work from this best-selling author team. It offers complete coverage le/ of two examination Courses, elementary & intermediate, 87 within one book, & its target student readership words/ is those people who aim for these ② stages.

TG/McGH/OP

Today's date

Unit 13

All the jobs in this unit are to be typed using the indented form of display and full punctuation.

Job 1 (266 words)

A4 bond paper.
Passage about open and full punctuation and abbreviations.
Use the indented form of display.
Centre the main heading: OPEN AND FULL PUNCTUATION, AND ABBREVIATIONS.
Other headings to be typed as shoulder headings in lower case and underscored.
Single spacing and margins of 19–88.

Job 2 (234 words)

A4 bond paper.
Passage about continuation sheets.
Centre the main and subheading: C O N T I N U A T I O N   S H E E T S
                                    Letters and Memoranda
Use the indented form of display and full punctuation.
Single spacing and margins of 19–88.

Job 3 (338 words)

Memo on A4 headed memo paper with a carbon copy on bank paper.
(Headed paper may be used from *AUDIO TRANSCRIPTION, TEACHER'S MANUAL.*)
From: Sales Manager   To: Managing Director
Ref: PRT/SMan/250/JMB   Date: 3 June 1985
Heading: SALES MEETING – 22 MAY 1985
Use the indented form of display and margins of 13–90.
A continuation sheet will be required.

Job 4 (53 words)

Memo on A5 headed memo paper with a carbon on bank paper.
(Headed paper may be used from *AUDIO TRANSCRIPTION, TEACHER'S MANUAL.*)
From: D. W. Bennett   To: Mr. J. Cornhill
Ref: DWB/BR   Date: Today's
Heading: ADVERTISEMENT Margins: 13–90
Use the indented form of display and full punctuation.
The following advertisement is to be incorporated in the memo:
CLEAN-CAR SERVICES LTD.
Trafalgar Street, Burnley, BB11 1LJ
specialize in providing a
RAPID and EFFICIENT
car-wash service
Book of 20 Vouchers – £15
(Valid Monday to Thursday only)
OPEN: 8 a.m. – 6 p.m. Monday to Saturday

Job 5 (48 words)

Memo on A5 headed memo paper with a carbon copy on bank paper.
(Headed paper may be used from *AUDIO TRANSCRIPTION, TEACHER'S MANUAL.*)
From: Winifred F. Salmons   To: Ms. J. P. Arrowsmith
Ref: WFS/uy   Date: 24 January 1985
Heading: BUDGET FOR THE YEAR ENDED 31 DECEMBER 1984
Use the indented form of display, full punctuation and margins of 13–90.

A4 bond paper.   Margins 22–82.

TAKE A NEW AND FRESH APPROACH WITH

TYPING: TWO-IN-ONE COURSE

Archie Drummond
Anne Coles-Mogford
with Ida Scattergood

One Course - Two Levels of Achievement

*   Clear and positive instructions

*   Well-planned, making use of time available

*   Full coverage of intermediate requirements

All the factors of a changing market and environment are taken
into account in this new work from this best-selling author
team. It offers complete coverage of two examination courses,
elementary and intermediate, within one book, and its target
readership is those people who aim for these two stages.

TG/McGH/OP

Today's date

Our Ref JR/Your initials

12 February 1985

The Manager
Excelsior Hotel
National Exhibition Centre
BIRMINGHAM
B36 2LJ

Dear Sir

This is to confirm that I have booked 2 single rooms (with shower) fac-
ing north - away from Birmingham airport - for the night of 11 March.
I hope to arrive in Birmingham about 1600 hours.

Please let me have confirmation of this reservation.

Yours faithfully
DOSSETT & PARNELL (INTERNATIONAL) LTD

John Roberts
Contracts and Service Manager

Unit 7

This unit is divided into 4 sections.

SECTION A Ten numbered sentences containing homophones. Use A4 paper with margins of 13 and 90 and single spacing. Each sentence should be typed on a separate line, and you must listen to a complete sentence before starting to type. When you still have 3 or 4 words to type, start listening to the next sentence.

SECTION B In Section B, page 39, read the information dealing with the use of the hyphen and dash. In Section C you will be asked to type sentences based on the explanations and examples given.

SECTION C

Exercise 1 A4 paper, margins 13–90 and single spacing. Fourteen numbered sentences incorporating the use of the comma, hyphen and dash. Each sentence starts on a separate line.

Exercise 2 (66 words) Two paragraphs on A5 landscape paper. Margins of 13–90 and single spacing. Emphasis on use of hyphen and dash.

Exercise 3 (75 words) Three paragraphs on A5 portrait paper. Margins of 13–63 and single spacing. Emphasis on hyphen and apostrophe.

SECTION D A5 letters with carbon copies (where indicated) and envelopes. Single spacing and margins 13–64.

Job 1 (97 words) From: Dossett & Parnell (International) Ltd,
26 High Street, Highbury, London, N5 1UD
(Headed paper may be used from *AUDIO TRANSCRIPTION, TEACHER'S MANUAL*)
To: F S Grommett, 26 Orchard Road, Witney, Oxon, OX8 7AW
Ref: DetP/487/RWD/P   Date: 25 September 1985
Subject heading: DETACHED PROPERTIES IN THE HIGHBURY AREA
Take one carbon copy and type a suitable envelope.

Job 2 (80 words) From: Roger G Hazel, Office Manager of Dossett & Parnell (International) Ltd,
26 High Street, Highbury, London, N5 1UD
(Headed paper may be used from *AUDIO TRANSCRIPTION, TEACHER'S MANUAL*)
To: The A1 Business Training Centre,
26 Adam Street, Carlisle, CA2 7JJ
Mark the letter FOR THE ATTENTION OF MISS A RHODES
Ref: RGH/WP/AB   Date: 10 October 1985
Take one carbon copy and type a suitable envelope.

Your Ref EC/NOV

Our Ref JR/Your initials

12 February 1985

Ms Elizabeth Campbell
President
County Association for Women
34 The Nook
BROADWAY
Worcs
WR12 7DW

Dear Ms Campbell

Thank you for your letter dated 8 February, and for the invitation to make an after-lunch speech to members of your association on Friday, 14 June, 1985.

I am very pleased to have been invited, I am happy to accept, and I shall be delighted to join you at 1230 hours for lunch at 1300.

I shall let you know the title of my talk in a week or so, and I most certainly shall have something to say about 'The Place of Trade Unions in Society'.

Yours sincerely

Job 3 (86 words)

From: Edward Brookes, Managing Director of
Dossett & Parnell (International) Ltd – address as in Job 2
(Headed paper may be used from *AUDIO TRANSCRIPTION, TEACHER'S MANUAL*)
To: Cheltenham Landscapes plc,
Dover Road, Cheltenham, Glos, GL50 1AA
Mark the letter FOR THE ATTENTION OF MR A HARTLEY-ROBINSON
Ref: EB/FGP   Date: 18 March 1985
Subject heading: LANDSCAPING OF GROUNDS TO FACTORY
Take one carbon copy and type a suitable envelope.

Job 4 (111 words)

From: Mrs Hilary Hewitt, District Commissioner of Guides,
Ivy House, The Crescent, Portsmouth, Hants, PO6 3AB
(Address to be typed at scale point 48.)
To: Regal Coaches Ltd, Selly Park, Portsmouth, Hants, PO2 9LA
Mark the letter FOR THE ATTENTION OF MR BERNARD RODGERS
Ref: HH/HOS   Date: 14 May 1985
Subject heading: COUNTY GUIDE RALLY – 7 SEPTEMBER 1985
Take one carbon copy and type a suitable envelope.

Our Ref   JR/Your initials

12 February 1985

Mr R Laurie
Stamford Office Agency
22 High Street
STAMFORD
Lincs
PE9 2AA

Dear Sir

Please send us a copy of your Salary Survey for Office Staff - 1984-1985.
Also, let us know the cost of the publication, and we will mail our
cheque by return.

We found last year's survey most useful, and if we can be of help with
the 1985-1986 survey, we will be happy to co-operate.

Yours faithfully
DOSSETT & PARNELL (INTERNATIONAL) LTD

John Roberts
Contracts and Service Manager

SECTION A

A4 paper.　　Margins 13–90.　　Single spacing.

```
 1  He was formerly principal of the technical college.
 2  He sent a letter formally accepting the invitation.
 3  The architect will visit the building site on 12 July.
 4  After the accident, John's sight deteriorated very rapidly.
 5  Make sure you check all the invoices before making payment.
 6  Cheques should be signed and despatched on the last day of May.
 7  The Five Choirs Festival is scheduled for the end of September.
 8  The lecturer told us that a quire of paper consisted of 24 sheets.
 9  In due course Mr John Jones will move to more up-to-date premises.
10  Although they dressed well, their clothes were made of coarse material.
```

SECTION B

I am going to give you guidance on when to use the hyphen and dash. There are few steadfast rules for the use of the hyphen and dash, and the ones that exist are inconsistent! The following suggestions should prove helpful.

THERE IS NO SPACE BEFORE OR AFTER A HYPHEN WHEN IT IS FULFILLING ITS FUNCTION OF DIVIDING OR JOINING WORDS OR SYLLABLES.

Look carefully at the 2 sentences that follow and see how they differ.
1　He was a hard working man. (No hyphen – a working man with a hard nature.)
2　He was a hard-working man. (A man who worked hard.)

The hyphen is used

NUMBER 1　　To divide a word at the end of a line; for example:
In word division at the end of a line, always be guided by the pro-nunciation of a word.

NUMBER 2　　To make clear the meaning of a word; for example:
recover and re-cover; reserve and re-serve.
We must re-elect the chairman at the next **AGM.**
The mid-Wales **Operatic Group will give a** concert tomorrow.
I have to de-ice the freezer.
We went motoring in **Inverness**-shire last autumn.
I **have** to go to hospital for a chest X-ray.

NUMBER 3　　In compound words before a noun, where 2 or more words are treated as one word; for example:
A country-wide, large-scale operation took place.
The equipment has a time-saving directory and black-on-white VDU.
The typewriter has an alpha-numeric keyboard and lift-off correction ribbon.

NOTE　If the expression comes after the noun, hyphens are not inserted; for example:
This is an up-to-date report. (Adjective describing report.)
This report has been brought up to date. (No hyphens – adverbial phrase modifying verb brought.)

NUMBER 4　　Between tens and units when words are used instead of figures in cardinal and ordinal numbers (21 to 99). Also, to express fractions in words; for example:
The principal lecturer was in his sixty-first year.
One-third of the business houses had microcomputers.
The price of this house is £72,225 (seventy-two thousand two hundred and twenty-five pounds).

Job 3 (b)   A5 headed paper.   Margins 13–63.   Single spacing.

```
Your Ref  KB/SC

Our Ref  JR/Your initials

12 February 1985

Miss K Baxter
R J Canning Ltd
11 Holly Tree Road
VENTNOR
Isle of Wight
PO38 2AZ

Dear Miss Baxter

Thank you for your letter, dated 11 February,
about the service contracts.

I shall be pleased to see you in my office here
on Monday next, 18 February, at 12 noon.  I look
forward to seeing you again, and I hope you will
have time to take lunch with me at the Allshires
Golf Club.

Yours sincerely
```

Job 4   A5 memo paper.   Margins 13–90.   Single spacing.

```
To    Joyce Delaney                    From  John Roberts

Date  12 February 1985                 Ref   JR/Your initials

Thank you for your memo, dated 7 February, about the new copying machines.

I should be pleased to see a demonstration and suggest Tuesday afternoon,
19 February.

I feel that the price is very high, and think you should obtain quotations
from sources other than Rank, Bayliss & Co.  I am certain the Board of
Directors will require at least 3 quotations.
```

NUMBER 5   To represent the word to; for example:
The company's address was 12-14 Paradise Street.
He lived from 1901-1976; or
He lived from 1901-76.
It was a Southampton-Santander crossing.

NUMBER 6   Sometimes with a colon; for example: Please supply the following items:–

NUMBER 7   In hypenated surnames and compound titles containing vice, ex, elect, for example:
Mr Hudson-Evans was appointed Vice-Chancellor of the university.
Mrs Constance Hay-Roxburgh is an ex-President of the Association.

NUMBER 8   To avoid repeating a word that is common to a number of elements, a hyphen is inserted and the word appears in the last compound only; for example:
All we have left is 2-, 3-, and 4-bedroomed flats.

In typewriting the DASH is represented by the same sign as the hyphen, BUT the dash has a space BEFORE and AFTER it. The HYPHEN LINKS 2 or more words. The DASH SEPARATES words/ideas.

The dash
is used

NUMBER 9   To show an abrupt change in thought; for example:
A strange noise was heard, and then – but I will not spoil the story.

NOTE If the original thought is continued after the interruption, another dash is necessary, as in the sentences which follow:
I believe – but I may be wrong – that the machine was deliberately broken.
A record number of exhibitors – more than 2,000 – were in the hall.

NUMBER 10   To indicate hesitant speech; for example:
'Oh – er – yes – I think so.'
'Well – perhaps – no – I don't know.'

NUMBER 11   To represent the minus sign; for example:
$7 - 4 = 3. 14 - 9 = 5. 14 - 17 = -3.$

NOTE To show a minus quantity, the dash (with a space before it) is placed close to the figure.

SECTION C

Exercise 1   A4 paper.   Margins 13–90.   Single spacing.

```
1   Please buy 4 2-way, 3-pin electric plugs.
2   The VDU screen displays easy-to-read text.
3   The money - all stolen - was hidden in the tree.
4   We guarantee free after-sales service for 5 years.
5   Even as a teenager, she was a pre-eminent disc jockey.
6   The information in the manual was certainly up to date.
7   In the Birmingham, Ladywood, by-election there was a re-count.
8   This electronic typewriter has a 2-line error correction memory.
9   At the biannual meeting of the Club he recounted his experiences.
10  This computer can be connected to a multi-feed processing system.
11  Queen Victoria (1819-1901) was the daughter of Edward, Duke of Kent.
12  There was a great deal of noise - both from the aircraft and the wind.
13  The object of the course was to prepare learners for predetermined jobs.
14  My cheque for £22,225 (twenty-two thousand two hundred and twenty-five
    pounds) was posted yesterday.
```

MAKING APPOINTMENTS

When dealing with appointments, keep the following objectives in mind:

1 give date, day, time, and place of meeting;
2 offer flexibility in setting date and time;
3 state reason for the appointment;
4 where possible, suggest the length of time required;
5 when confirming an appointment, always restate the day, date, and hour
   of the appointment so that there is no misunderstanding.

BRIEF NOTES

When you have to compose from brief notes, always:

1 type a rough copy of the notes; the message should be word for word,
   exactly as it was dictated, so that you can see clearly what was said;
2 use double spacing and margins of 20 and 80;
3 as this first typing is only a rough copy, it is a waste of time to correct errors: just leave them;
4 remove your typescript from the machine and with a pen or pencil make
   any alterations necessary;
5 avoid short, disconnected sentences;
6 decide on margins that you will use for the final typing;
7 insert a sheet of paper and type the message again, setting it out as
   you want it to look when finished; for example, in a business letter you
   would put in the reference, date, name and address of addressee, salutation, etc - do not bother to correct typing errors;
8 remove paper from machine and read very carefully what you have typed,
   making any further amendments that may be necessary;
9 insert a fresh sheet of paper, with appropriate carbon copies, and type
   final copy ready for despatch;
10 proofread carefully and correct any typing errors neatly, before removing the paper from the machine, and make sure that you produce a clean,
   mailable copy.

Job 3 (a)   Corrected rough draft.   Margins used in rough draft 20–80.
                       Double spacing.

Dear Miss Baxter   *,dated 11 February,*

~~Letter to Kay Baxter:~~ Thank you for your letter/about the

N.P.   service contracts. [I shall be pleased to see you in my office

          here on Mon*d*y next ~~(put in date)~~ *,18 February,* at 12 noon. I look forward

          to seeing you again, / I hope ~~she~~ *you* will have time to take lunch
                                                            and

          with me at the Allshires Golf Club. *Yours sincerely* ~~I will sign the letter.~~

                       (See next page for displayed letter)

Exercise 2   A5 landscape paper.   Margins 13–90.   Single spacing.

```
Michael Sullivan, great-grandson of the founder, was only 31 years
of age when he was re-elected - by virtue of his far-sighted views -
Managing Director of the Company.

The Company is moving its factory - now old and dilapidated - to
new premises where up-to-date machinery has been installed.  The
factory makes ready-to-wear suits of first-class quality and up-
to-the-minute style.
```

Exercise 3   A5 portrait paper.   Margins 13–63.   Single spacing.

```
Please send us 6 1-kilo tins of brilliant white
emulsion paint, and 5 2-kilo tins of weather-
resisting gloss paint.

The above-named shop is holding - in 10 days'
time - a one-week sale of fire-damaged ladies',
men's, and children's clothing of high-grade
quality.

John said that he was starting in 2 weeks' time on
a fortnight's cruise, but we are now told that he
is taking his daughter's youngest child abroad in
his son's car.
```

COMPOSING MEMOS AND LETTERS - GENERAL HINTS

1 TONE The tone should suit the occasion. If your employer is answering a complaint from a customer, he will not say, 'We fail to understand why you are complaining.' He will say, 'We are not clear as to why you are making a complaint', or similar wording. If your Managing Director writes to a customer asking him/her to change an appointment, he will not say, 'I must ask you to change your appointment to next Tuesday, 21 May.' He will say, 'I am very sorry that it will not be possible to keep the appointment you made for Tuesday, 21 May, because . . . and I wonder if you would be kind enough to suggest another date and time.' Similarly, if your Managing Director was writing to his Works Manager asking him to change an appointment, he would probably say, 'I am sorry that I have to cancel our meeting for 0930 hours on Monday, 27 May; instead I would like to see you at 1100 hours on Tuesday, 28 May.'

2 THINK OF THE READER Someone once said that the difference between a good business letter and a bad one was the difference between 'we' and 'you'. The reader of a letter is usually concerned with his own point of view: 'You will be pleased to know' is better than 'We are pleased to tell you'. If your chairman is unable to accept an invitation, his reply would always be courteous although the tone would vary depending on the circumstances. He would never say, 'Mr Black regrets he cannot accept your invitation.' He would say something like, 'Mr Black was pleased to receive your invitation and wishes very much that he could accept, but . . .'

3 BE CONCISE Get to the point immediately you start a letter or memo. If there has been previous correspondence, say so and give dates, and also say what the correspondence was about.

4 CHECK FOR ACCURACY See that all the statements are accurate. Much time and money are lost in offices each year just because facts are not checked. Misspelling the name of the addressee is an unforgivable error, and if you use the wrong date or a wrong number, this may distort or completely change the meaning of the letter. Do not sacrifice accuracy for the small amount of time it takes to verify facts.

Job 1 A5 headed portrait paper. A5 bank paper. Margins 13–64.

Ref DetP/487/RWD/P

25 September 1985

Mr F S Grommett
26 Orchard Road
WITNEY
Oxon OX8 7AW

Dear Mr Grommett

DETACHED PROPERTIES IN THE HIGHBURY AREA

Thank you for your letter of 16 September.

I enclose details of 6 properties in Highbury and
district for your consideration. May I particularly
draw your attention to the Old School House which is
slightly larger than you are requesting but which
has a pleasant garden and overlooks Highbury Fields.
It is available for £59,800 and I urge you to view,
as it has many distinctive features.

I can arrange to be at our offices to discuss the
properties with you, on any of your visits to this
area.

Yours sincerely

R W DOSSETT
Manager

Encs

Job 2 A5 headed portrait paper.

Ref RGH/WP/AB

10 October 1985

FOR THE ATTENTION OF MISS A RHODES

The A1 Business Training Centre
26 Adam Street
CARLISLE
CA2 7JJ

Dear Sirs

My firm is changing to a system of word processing
in the Export Department.

I am writing to enquire whether your Business Training Centre can provide a course for 6 of our staff
whose names and qualifications are attached.

We would like them all to attend this course before
November to give our staff sufficient time to become
accustomed to the new procedures before the system
is installed early in 1986.

Yours faithfully

ROGER G HAZEL
OFFICE MANAGER

Att

Unit 12

In this unit we are going to look at the art of composing memos and letters from brief notes.

You have to assume that all the brief notes have been dictated by John Roberts, Contracts and Service Manger, Dossett & Parnell (International) Ltd, who will sign all the letters. The reference is JR/Your own initials. Take a carbon copy of all letters. Date the letters and the memos 12 February 1985 – a Tuesday. Where a letter ends Yours sincerely, do not add name of company, name of writer or his designation. When a letter ends Yours faithfully, type the name of the organization (DOSSETT & PARNELL (INTERNATIONAL) LTD), turn up a minimum 5 spaces and then type the writer's name with his designation on the next line.

Job 1 (500 words)

Advice about composing memos and letters. A4 plain bond paper, margins 13 and 90 and single spacing. There is a main heading and paragraph headings. In this job you are asked to type ellipses (omission of words from a sentence), and you should insert the usual 3 spaced dots.

Job 2 (216 words)

Advice about making business appointments and composing memos and letters from brief notes. A4 plain bond paper, margins 13 and 90 and single spacing. There is a main heading, a shoulder heading and 2 groups of numbered items – the second group is numbered 1–10.

Job 3 (75 words)

On page 67 you will find the brief notes dicated by John Roberts in reply to a letter (dated 11 February 1985) from Miss Kay Baxter, R J Canning Ltd, 11 Holly Tree Road, Ventnor, Isle of Wight, PO38 2AZ. The salutation is Dear Miss Baxter. The reference on Miss Baxter's letter is KB/SC.

Job 4 (70 words)

This memo is from John Roberts to Joyce Delaney and is about a quotation from Rank, Bayliss & Co. Joyce Delaney's memo was dated 7 February 1985.

Job 5 (80 words)

This letter is from John Roberts to Mr R Laurie, Stamford Office Agency, 22 High Street, Stamford, Lincs, PE9 2AA. It is about Salary Survey for Office Staff – 1984–1985. The salutation is Dear Sir.

Job 6 (120 words)

This is a letter from John Roberts to Ms Elizabeth Campbell, President, County Association for Women, 34 The Nook, Broadway, Worcs, WR12 7DW. Ms Campbell's letter was dated 8 February 1985, and her reference is EC/NOV. John Roberts has been asked to give an after-lunch talk to the County Association, and he tells Ms Campbell that he will have something to say about 'The Place of Trade Unions in Society'.

Job 7 (60 words)

Here John Roberts asks you to write, for his signature, to the Excelsior Hotel, National Exhibition Centre, Birmingham, B36 2LJ.

Job 3   A5 headed portrait paper.   A5 bank paper.   Margins 13—64.

Ref EB/FGP

18 March 1985

FOR THE ATTENTION OF MR A HARTLEY—ROBINSON

Cheltenham Landscapes plc
Dover Road
CHELTENHAM
Glos
GL50 1AA

Dear Sirs

LANDSCAPING OF GROUNDS TO FACTORY

I am anxious to arrange for an area around my factory
to be landscaped following the completion of an
extension to the factory.

The site contains 3 mature trees and has a natural
slope of some 30 square yards.

I would value the advice of your consultant landscaper,
and I wonder if it would be possible for him to telephone my secretary to arrange for him to visit the site,
which is approximately 3 acres.

Yours faithfully

EDWARD BROOKES
Managing Director

Job 4   A5 portrait paper.   A5 bank paper.   Margins 13—64.

(48)
Ivy House
The Crescent
PORTSMOUTH
Hants PO6 3AB

Ref HH/HOS

14 May 1985

FOR THE ATTENTION OF MR BERNARD RODGERS

Regal Coaches Ltd
Selly Park
PORTSMOUTH
Hants PO2 9LA

Dear Sirs

COUNTY GUIDE RALLY – 7 SEPTEMBER 1985

I am anxious to arrange transport for 300 guides
and guiders from Portsmouth to attend the County
Guide Rally which is to be held at the Wavell Park,
Winchester, on Saturday, 7 September 1985. I am
enclosing a map of the Park area.

The Rally is due to begin at 1430 hours, and we
would need to arrive at the Park no later than
1300 hours. I anticipate that we would be ready
to leave Winchester at approximately 1800 hours.

I should be glad if you would give me a quotation
for the above transport.

Yours faithfully

Mrs Hilary Hewitt
District Commissioner of Guides

Enc

SUMNER JACOBS PLC

Summer Dresses & Jacobs Separates Spring
                                    Collections

PASTEL SUNDAES

Left: SUMNER pastel stripe sundress
Style No: 1900
Fabric Content: 100% cotton

UC

Colourways: Blue/Pink/Grey, turquoise/Grey/
                        Lemon, Grey/Pink/Peach
Sizes: 10-16
Wholesale Price: £7.95

} single spacing

Right: SUMNER pastel stripe skirt w.
                        side pockets & belt

Style No: 52323
Fabric Content: 100% cotton
Colourways: (as above)
Sizes: 10-16
Wholesale Price: £5.95

} single spacing

For further information please contact Liz Watson

EW/S/12
date

(Please type on A5
landscape. No cc/
required)

Unit 8

This unit is divided into 4 sections.

SECTION A   Ten numbered sentences containing words that may be difficult to spell. Use A4 paper with margins of 13 and 90 and single spacing. Each sentence must be typed on a separate line, and you must listen to a complete sentence before starting to type. When you still have 3 or 4 words to type, start listening to the next sentence.

SECTION B   In Section B, page 46, read the information dealing with the use of brackets and single/double quotes. In Section C you will be asked to type sentences based on the explanations and examples given.

SECTION C   Use same paper as in Section A. Ten numbered sentences incorporating the use of brackets and quotation marks. Each sentence starts on a separate line.

SECTION D   A4 letters with carbon copies and envelopes. Single spacing and margins 19–88.

Job 1 (207 words)
From: Dossett & Parnell (International) Ltd,
26 High Street, Highbury, London, N5 1UD
(Headed paper may be used from *AUDIO TRANSCRIPTION, TEACHER'S MANUAL*)
To: Sq Ldr F J Eames AFC, Entertainments Officer, RAF Bournbrook, Yeovil, Somerset, BA20 8HX
Ref: PJC/TE   Date: 23 October 1985
Subject heading: CHRISTMAS PARTY AT LONSDALE ROAD COMMUNITY CENTRE
This letter incorporates simple displayed matter.
Take one carbon copy and type an envelope.
Change all times to 24-hour clock.

Job 2 (197 words)
From: Dossett & Parnell, etc
(Headed paper may be used from *AUDIO TRANSCRIPTION, TEACHER'S MANUAL*)
To : T M Farrell Esq OBE, 192 South Street, Winchester, Hants, SO23 8UJ
Our ref: DF/12/JP   Your ref: TF/HL   Date: 19 November 1985
Subject heading: PROMOTION VISIT TO THE USSR
Take 2 carbon copies and type an envelope.

Job 3 (215 words)
From: Arrow Training Centre, Greenford, Middlesex, UB6 8AA
(Address to be typed at scale point 66.)
To: All Head Teachers   Ref: A/ATA&C/23/3/2 FTBB
Date: January 1985
Subject heading: CAMPS AND COURSES
This letter will be photocopied; there is no need to take a carbon copy.
The envelopes will be typed later.

Unit 11
Office-style dictation

Unit 11

PREPARATORY SENTENCES

These sentences will not be dictald, and you should type them through at least once, paying particular attention to the spelling. The sentences are designed to help you with some of the more difficult spellings and points of English in the office-style dictation.

1 His appointment was scheduled for mid-March.
2 All members of staff will receive an annual personal appraisal.
3 Each parcel will be weighed separately.
4 He thought that commuting to London would be out of the question.
5 His predecessor had left the post some months previously.
6 The assistant cut her waist-length hair into loose, soft layers.

OFFICE-STYLE DICTATION

You are audio typist to Liz Watson, a director of Sumner Jacobs plc. The company is involved in the design, manufacture and distribution of clothing.

Insert references as indicated by the dictator and take a file copy of each task, unless instructed otherwise. Date each piece of dictation 17 May 1986.

(a) Letter of 100 words to Mrs C Harper, SPS Superstores plc, Market Street, Oxford, OX1 3SE.

(b) Memorandum of 90 words to Gerald Simpson.
Subject heading: Style No 551 – Khaki Jumpsuit

(c) Letter of 190 words to Mrs P Wharton, 22b Germyn Street, Southport, Merseyside, PR9 6YY.

(d) Passage of 299 words headed: Paris Fashion – 6–8 March.

(e) Manuscript to be typed on A5 landscape paper.

Names and words other than those given above:

Mexican
Rosalie James
T-shirts
swatch
Richmond
cropped trousers

RECOMMENDED TRANSCRIPTION TIME: 2 hours

Job 4   Type a page from the brochure, which is to be attached to the previous letter, displaying it attractively on A4 bond paper.

**Manuscript referred to
in (f) and to
accompany (e)**

Display this on A5 portrait paper

TOP CLASS SEC/PA

req'd by expanding Market Research agency,
as assistant to senior consultant.

Good shorthand/typing skills (100/60), &
ability to liaise confidently at all levels
essential.

Knowledge of foreign langs, particularly
German, and/or w.processing experience,
useful.

Salary circa £6500

Pls. send CV to;

Mr R Berrington
Iconi Associates
Lodge House
Lord St.... (pls complete)

double spacing

```
 1  Did you achieve the goal you set yourself?
 2  Please send me 2 of your new woollen jumpers.
 3  It is advisable for you to leave on the early ferry.
 4  I am dissatisfied with the result of the competition.
 5  I will need a 1986 calendar by the beginning of August.
 6  The symphony concert was excellent from beginning to end.
 7  Our Marketing Director requires an efficient audio typist.
 8  The management conceded that the union's demand was reasonable.
 9  I agreed that a quorum of 8 was, in the circumstances, not unreasonable.
10  The gardener had infinite patience, but he took a long time to finish the
    job.
```

SECTION B

Today I am going to give you guidance on when to use brackets and single and double quotes.

Left and right brackets (parentheses)

The comma, dash and brackets are 3 ways of marking off additional or incidental remarks. The brackets are the strongest of these 3 punctuation marks, but there are no hard and fast rules about when one would be preferable to the other 2.

Brackets are used

NUMBER 1   To enclose letters, words or expressions that are independent of the main thought of the sentence; for example:
The majority of the members present (about 65 per cent) were against the motion.
The previous edition (1982) sold more copies.

NUMBER 2   To enclose letters, or numbers, when these are used to identify listed items in a sentence and in enumerations; for example:
Accurate typing depends on: (a) concentration, (b) correct posture.
(1) For an explanation of the use of the brace (continuous brackets) see *TYPING: TWO-IN-ONE COURSE,* page 93.

Quotation marks

There are double quotes (inverted commas) and single quotes (the apostrophe). Modern practice appears to favour single quotes, and we shall use this method in *AUDIO TRANSCRIPTION,* although there is no reason why double quotes should not be used. For a quotation within a quotation, we shall use double quotes within single quotes, but, here again, there is no reason why double quotes should not be used outside and single quotes inside. You MUST BE CONSISTENT.

Quotation marks are used

NUMBER 3   To enclose the exact words of a speaker or writer; for example:
'Please tell me that story again', he said.
The Office Manager said, 'All typists must use electronic typewriters.'

NOTE   It is modern practice to use a colon and no quotation marks when giving a complete quotation; for example:
The Office Manager said: All typists must use electronic typewriters.

NUMBER 4   To enclose the titles of articles, plays, lectures, poems, songs, etc; for example:
Please order the book, 'Typing First Course'.
I have read the book 'Cold is the Sea' many times.

NOTE   (1) Punctuation marks may be placed before or after the quotes, depending on the sense of the sentence; for example:

Unit 10
Office-style dictation

PREPARATORY SENTENCES

These sentences will not be dictated, and you should type them through at least once, paying particular attention to the spelling. The sentences are designed to help you with some of the more difficult spellings and points of English in the office-style dictation.

1 Unfortunately, we had to postpone the party.
2 The buffet, at £5.00 a head, was excellent.
3 He appointed a manager of low calibre.
4 The group of ladies were all non-smokers.
5 Incidentally, what was the attitude of the candidates?
6 It is our mutual wish to find an alternative date, as we both have other commitments.

OFFICE-STYLE DICTATION

You are audio typist to Mrs Margaret D Edgwood, Market Research Consultant at ICONI ASSOCIATES. Make a carbon copy of each document typed. Date all documents 3 May 1986. Use reference MDE/your initials.

(a)

A letter of 124 words to Mr B Collingwood, 56 Yew Tree Lane, Bradford, West Yorkshire, BD7 0TY.
Subject heading: MARKET RESEARCH SOCIETY – ACORN

(b)

Memorandum of 172 words to Mrs M Knight.
Subject heading: HALL TESTS – PARKWAY COOKERS

(c)

A letter of 188 words to RSM plc, Hebdon Works, West Road, Halifax, West Yorkshire, HX4 6BM, marked for the attention of Mr O Venters, Marketing Department.

(d)

A letter of 65 words to Mr J R Ewing, 94 Green Valley Road, Hall Green, Birmingham, B28 7QR.
Subject Heading: IZI HANOVER GMBH

(e)

A memorandum of 95 words to Mr R Berrington.
Subject heading: REPLACEMENT FOR THERESA CROSS

(f)

Accompanying manuscript to be typed on A5 paper.

Names and words other than those given above:

Bill Miller
Central Hall, Liverpool
external catering firm
chemicals in manufacturing cosmetics
questionnaires
liaise

RECOMMENDED TRANSCRIPTION TIME: 2 hours

She asked, 'Did you see the play "The Mousetrap"?'
I wonder why she said, 'Am I included?'
Do you know why she said, 'What a dreadful party'?

(2) The use of the underscore for book titles, names of plays, lectures, etc, wastes time and is not now popular.

(3) There seems to be no good reason why book titles, etc, should not be typed in closed capitals; for example:
'Did you see the play THE MOUSETRAP?'

(4) Many newspapers type book titles, etc, with initial capitals and without quotation marks; for example:
'Did you see the play The Mousetrap?'

NUMBER 5   To enclose matter that is quoted from another source. If there is one paragraph only, quotation marks are put at the beginning and end of the paragraph. If there is more than one paragraph, the quotes are typed at the BEGINNING of EACH paragraph and at the END of the LAST paragraph.

NUMBER 6   To enclose verses of poetry. The quotes are put at the beginning of the FIRST verse and at the end of the LAST verse.

NUMBER 7   To enclose special interpretation, slang words or words used in a different sense from their original meaning; for example:
She smiled and said, 'You want to "get with it".'
Deliver all the documents marked 'Urgent'.

NOTE   What was at one time considered an 'unusual' word, or slang, may quite easily become part of our language and quotation marks would be no longer used.

SECTION C   Paper used in Section A.

```
 1  Why did you say to him 'Am I late?'
 2  Margaret said, 'Call and see me tomorrow.'
 3  Why did you say to him 'Look behind you'?
 4  Please fetch me a copy of the Daily Herald.
 5  We watch Spaceman's Mission every Thursday.
 6  The Americans celebrate Independence Day (4 July) every year.
 7  Both ports (Dover and Harwich) were closed because of a strike.
 8  The chairman said: The Board of Directors will meet on 21 January.
 9  Write the words 'By Hand' in the top right corner of the envelope.
10  Please send me copies of (a) Audio Transcription and (b) Applied Typing.
```

A4 bond paper.   Margins 19–88.

```
W I L S O N S    L I M I T E D

193/4 Broad Street  MORPETH  Northumberland   NE61 1AA

Telephone: 0670 22475
```

<u>Main PANTHER Agents</u>

```
SERVICING DEPARTMENT
```

Six good reasons why you should have your vehicle serviced at
WILSONS

I   Our Servicing Department is a small Department that does not
      have the high costs and overheads of major distributors.
      This is reflected in our charge rates which are highly com-
      petitive and certainly less than major distributors.

II   The service that you will receive is completely personal. If
      you want to see and discuss the work that has been done on
      your vehicle, you are absolutely welcome to do so.

III   Our Servicing Department is centrally located and we have a
      courtesy car service available to drop you at your local place
      of employment after you have booked your car in.

IV   Our mechanics have been on the appropriate manufacturers' courses
      and are highly-skilled men.

V   We have full MOT test facilities available.

VI   We have the most up-to-date diagnostic equipment available.

PR/JCM/424

26 February 1985
```
```

Job 1　　　　　　　　　A4 headed bond paper.　A4 bank paper.　Envelope.　Margins 19–88.

PJC/TE

23 October 1985

Sq Ldr F J Eames AFC
Entertainments Officer
RAF Bournbrook
YEOVIL
Somerset
BA20 8HX

Dear Sir

CHRISTMAS PARTY AT LONSDALE ROAD COMMUNITY CENTRE

I am Chairman of our Management Committee, and Councillor Mrs J King
has told me of the concert party which has been created by the RAF
personnel at your base, and what excellent entertainment they provide.

I am in the process of arranging the entertainment for our annual
Christmas party, for the elderly of this district, which is to be held
on one of the following dates:

Saturday, 12 December at 1200 hours, or
Saturday, 19 December at 1200 hours

We shall be holding the party at the community centre, and expect a
turn-out of approximately 250 old people, plus helpers. The meal starts
at 1230 hours and after speeches by the Mayor and Councillor Mrs King,
it should be over by 1345 hours.

In previous years, we have had some form of entertainment from 1400 hours
to 1530 hours, and we would be delighted if the RAF concert party from
Bournbrook could entertain our senior citizens this year. On previous
occasions they have found particular pleasure in the singing of old
songs, and appreciated acts by a magician. I am sure the programme,
which I understand you provide, would be very well received.

I look forward to hearing from you.

Yours faithfully

Mrs P J Clowes
Managing Director

WILSONS LIMITED ← Spaced Caps

193/4 Broad St MORPETH Northumberland NE61 1AA
Telephone: 0670 22475

<u>Main PANTHER Agents</u>
Servicing Department ← uc

Six good reasons why y shld hv yr vehicle serviced at WILSONS

uc/ 1 Our <u>servicing department</u> is a small dept th does not hv the high costs + overheads of major distributors. This is reflected in our charge rates wh are highly competitive + certainly less than major distributors.

local h 2 Our Servicing Dept is centrally located + we hv a courtesy car service available to drop you at yr place of employment after you hv booked yr car in.

3 The service th you wl receive is completely personal. If you want to see o discuss the work th has been done on yr vehicle, you are absolutely welcome to do so.

4 Our mechanics hv bn on the appropriate manufacturers' courses + are highly-skilled men.

5 We hv full MOT test facilities available. DIAGNOSTIC

6 We hv the most up-to-date diagnostic equipment available.

TYPIST: Please change arabic figures to roman numerals

Ref
Date

Our ref   DF/12/JP

Your ref   TF/HL

19 November 1985

T M Farrell Esq OBE
192 South Street
WINCHESTER
Hants
SO23 8UJ

Dear Mr Farrell

PROMOTION VISIT TO THE USSR

Further to your visit to the USSR early in the New Year, I give below
the following additional information.

1 Payment Please complete and return the form attached to this
letter, enclosing a non-returnable deposit of £50 and 2 stamped, self-
addressed envelopes. The balance will be due 4 weeks before departure.

2 Passports If you do not possess a valid passport, please apply for
one at once by obtaining the relevant form from either a main Post
Office or from the Passport Office, Clive House, Petty France, London,
SW1 1AA.

3 Preparatory Meeting You will be invited to attend a preparatory
meeting in London where any final information will be given. This will
be an opportunity for all members of the group to meet together.

4 Insurance It is recommended that you take out insurance for this
visit, and you should indicate on the acceptance form whether you
require immediate cover. The insurance guarantees the return of your
deposit should you have to withdraw for medical or similarly serious
reasons.

Further information on visas (which we obtain on your behalf) will be
enclosed with our next letter.

Yours sincerely

Darrell Fitzpatrick
Director

Enc

A4 headed bond paper.   A4 bank paper.   Single spacing.
Margins 19–88.

PR/JCM/424

26 February 1985

Ms F Carter
26 Avenue Road
Rothbury
MORPETH
Northumberland
NE65 7SE

Dear Ms Carter

PANTHER 424

In September 1982 we had the pleasure of selling you a new car, and we
trust that this car has given you satisfactory service.

We are, at the moment, looking for good used cars such as yours to buy
outright for cash, and if you contemplate selling, we would certainly
be very interested.

Alternatively, if you are looking for an up-market, slightly larger car,
**we would be very pleased to take your car in part-exchange for a new
car from the fabulous Panther range.** Why not come and see (and roadtest) the outstanding Panther 424, 1300 cc range of hatchbacks or
saloons? For RELIABILITY, SPECIFICATION, QUALITY and VALUE they are
unbeatable. The normal specification on a Panther includes:

1 5-speed gearbox
2 **rear seat-belts**
3 electronic ignition.

Call in and see us, whether you are simply interested in selling your car
for cash, or whether you wish to roadtest a Panther 424; either way you
will be most welcome.

Yours sincerely

P RUSHTON
Managing Director

Enc

(66)
Arrow Training Centre
GREENFORD
Middlesex
UB6 8AA

Our ref   A/ATA&C/23/3/2 FTBB

January 1985

To all Head Teachers

Dear Sir/Madam

CAMPS AND COURSES

Every year a number of camps and courses are arranged during the summer
vacation. It is hoped that pupils will profit from attending one of
these camps or courses by becoming better members of the community
through the training and experience they receive.

Camps

The camps give young people a chance to exercise leadership and respons-
ibility, and also improve their general fitness. They are arranged to
coincide with the school holidays and last about one week.

Courses

Courses are also of about one week's duration, but are held throughout
the year. There are courses during the summer vacation if it is not
possible for pupils to have leave of absence during term time. The
courses cover a wide range of topics to broaden the individual's
interests and to help in preparation for the adult world.

I am enclosing a brochure giving full details of dates, times, venues,
and costs of the camps and courses for 1985. I appreciate that the
dates for camps and courses will not always be convenient to you, but
I hope that, whenever possible, you will do your best to allow your
pupils to attend, or to take their holidays to coincide with this
training.

Yours faithfully

Education Officer

Enc

M E M O R A N D U M

From Managing Director

To Manager, Staff Canteen

Date Today's

COMPLAINTS REGARDING THE STAFF CANTEEN

My attention has been drawn to the number of complaints regarding the canteen, and I would value your comments on them. Some were raised at a Staff Association Meeting, and others have come to my notice through individual complaints.

For convenience I list them, but not in any order of priority.

1 The sandwiches that are available at tea time are said to be somewhat stale.

2 The soup, although satisfactory as to taste, is often not hot; this may be due to it being served in cold dishes.

3 There are still a number of persons who use the canteen who are smoking, despite the 'No Smoking' notices that are displayed. I think you, or one of your senior staff, should approach these people when they are transgressing.

4 Are you certain that the prices for sweets are justifiable, particularly the following:

(i)   apple pie, £0.80
(ii)   rice pudding, £0.70
(iii) fruit salad, £1.00
(iv)   biscuits and cheese, £0.90?

As you know, the Board is anxious that the canteen should be well used by our staff in order that it should pay its way, and we need at least 300 people at each lunch-time sitting, or it will not be economically viable. I believe, in fact, that the number has dropped in the last 6 months to something like 250.

This is, therefore, an important matter, and I look forward to receiving your report on the points I have raised above.

I am enclosing some of the letters of complaint I have received from individual members of staff.

MD/SC/1

Encs

MONKTON

Monkton Gliding & Outdoor Activities Centre ← uc

GLIDING

All-inclusive 5-day holiday courses.

Book early for the best weeks.

Professional instructors w long experience of training beginners & early solo pilots.

WINCH Unique winch launching system for rapid turn round & max. flying time.

OTHER OUTDOOR ACTIVITIES

Golf
Fishing
Swimming
Riding
Hill Walking
Water Skiing
Archery
Sailing

TYPIST: 2 columns, please — of equal length

Expert tuition given in all the above activities. Courses held throughout the year.
Write for course brochures & further details to

The Manager
Monkton Gliding & Outdoor Activities Centre
ABOYNE
Aberdeenshire AB3 5EJ
Telephone: 0339 76229

TYPIST: Please insert reference & date

HOUSE FOR SALE

<u>Worcestershire</u>

An outstanding south-facing Regency house for sale
with magnificent views across Herefordshire to the
Black Mountains.   The house stands in about 1½ acres
of garden, and has the following accommodation:

(i)   Fine panelled hall, drawing room, sitting room,
dining room, playroom/study, 5 bedrooms, 2 bathrooms,
and 2 good attic rooms.

(ii)   Oil-fired central heating.

(iii)   Double glazing throughout.

(iv)   Outside there is a tennis court, swimming pool,
and a small paddock.

Offers in the region of £125,000, freehold, will be
considered.

A4 bond paper.   Margins 22–78.

MONKTON GLIDING AND OUTDOOR ACTIVITIES CENTRE

GLIDING

All-inclusive 5-day holiday courses.

Book early for the best weeks.

Professional instructors with long experience of training
beginners and early solo pilots.

Unique winch launching system for rapid turn round and
maximum flying time.

OTHER OUTDOOR ACTIVITIES
                    (39)
Golf   Hill Walking

Fishing   Water Skiing

Swimming   Archery

Riding   Sailing

Expert tuition given in all the above activities.   Courses
held throughout the year.

Write for course brochures and further details to

The Manager
Monkton Gliding and Outdoor Activities Centre
ABOYNE
Aberdeenshire   AB3 5EJ

Telephone: 0339 76229

A/ATA&C/23/3/2 FTBB

January 1985

Job 1 A4 bond paper. Single spacing. Margins 19—88.

YELLOW PAGES

Yellow Pages is a directory of business addresses and telephone
numbers compiled and published by British Telecom, and distributed
free to all telephone customers.

Each volume covers a different area and aims to make it as easy as
possible for the people in that area to find the goods and services
they need.

How to use Yellow Pages

I   To find the business or service you want - like 'Banks', for
example - just go through the Business Classifications using the page
headings until you find the right page. The Classifications are
listed alphabetically.

II   If you are not sure how a business or service is listed, use the
Classifications Index at the back of the book.

III Once you have found the right page, go through the list until
you find the business or service you are looking for. It may be one
you know, or the one that is closest to where you live. If you are
not sure which one to choose, see if any of them tell you more about
themselves in the advertisements.

Unit 9

The unit is divided into 4 sections.

SECTION A Ten numbered sentences containing homophones. Use A4 paper with margins of 13 and 90 and single spacing. Each sentence should be typed on a separate line, and you must listen to a complete sentence before starting to type. When you still have 3 or 4 words to type, start listening to the next sentence.

SECTION B In Section B, page 54, read the information dealing with the use of the semicolon and colon. In Section C you will be asked to type sentences based on the explanations and examples given.

SECTION C Use the same paper as in Section A. Eight numbered sentences incorporating the use of the semicolon and colon. Each sentence starts on a separate line. Watch carefully for the use of the apostrophe, the comma and the dash.

SECTION D The following 5 jobs are varied but each contains enumerated items, mainly using roman numerals.

Job 1 (182 words) A4 bond paper. Margins 19 and 88.
A passage in single spacing listing information about how to use Yellow Pages. Three enumerated items in capital roman numerals. Use double spacing between the enumerated items.

Job 2 (89 words) A5 portrait bond paper. Margins 13 and 64.
A passage in double spacing about a house for sale in Worcestershire. Four enumerated items in lower case roman numerals with brackets.

Job 3 (272 words) Memo on A4 headed memo paper with carbon copy on bank paper. Margins 13 and 90.
From: Managing Director   To: Manager, Staff Canteen
Heading: COMPLAINTS REGARDING THE STAFF CANTEEN
Ref: MD/SC/1   Date: Today's
Two groups of enumerated items numbered 1 to 4 in arabic figures and i to iv in bracketed small roman numerals.

Job 4 (169 words) Letter on A4 headed paper with carbon copy on bank paper. Margins 19 and 88.
From: Dossett & Parnell (International) Ltd, 26 High Street, Highbury, London, N5 1UD
To: Ms F Carter, 26 Avenue Road, Rothbury, Morpeth, Northumberland, NE65 7SE
Heading: PANTHER 424   Ref: PR/JCM/424   Date: 26 February 1985
Type an envelope of suitable size for the enclosure.

Job 5 (159 words) A4 bond paper. Margins 19 and 88.
Type, from manuscript copy in your book, the enclosure to be attached to the above letter.

SECTION A   A4 paper.   Margins 13–90.   Single spacing.

```
 1  We motor past your office building each morning at approximately 10.30.
 2  Has your sister passed the first stage of the word processing examination?
 3  I will send you a copy of the fourth edition of my book Applied Typing.
 4  In addition, the external memory allows you to store every document.
 5  The town council will meet to discuss the Mayor's radical proposals.
 6  You are advised to accept his counsel and buy the deserted building site.
 7  Will you hire a van in which to move your household furniture to Spain?
 8  The current of hot air carried the eagle higher and higher into space.
 9  A recent strike had a very serious effect on our production of new models.
10  The new machinery coming on to the market will affect our future plans.
```

SECTION B

The semicolon is used when the parts of a sentence need a stronger mark of separation than the comma.

The semicolon is used

NUMBER 1   To separate clauses of a compound sentence that are not joined by a conjunction or where the second clause is a conclusion or inference to be drawn from the first; for example:
Let us have the documents immediately; we cannot wait any longer.
There was prosperity everywhere; house prices were very high.

NUMBER 2   To separate independent clauses if they are connected by such words as 'consequently', 'however', 'therefore', 'accordingly', 'nevertheless', etc; for example:
Growth was at a standstill; however, it rained on St Swithin's Day!

NUMBER 3   Before such items as names and addresses, commodities and their prices, persons and their offices, etc, when these are in paragraph form, and when data between the items are separated by commas; for example:
We have offices in Newport, Gwent; Newport, Shropshire; and Newport, Dyfed.
The committee elected for the following year were: Chairman, Frank Daly; Secretary, Bruce Williamson; Treasurer, Peggy Osborne.

The colon is a mark of introduction and is used to

NUMBER 4   Introduce a list of items; for example:
Qualities looked for in an audio typist are: accuracy, speed, dependability and common sense.
We require the following: 2 pica daisywheels, 3 reams white bond A4.

NUMBER 5   Introduce a quotation; for example:
The Managing Director said: All prices must rise by 3 per cent.

NOTE   Notice the use of a capital letter after the colon in the last sentence. It was often the case that after the words 'as follows', a colon and hyphen were inserted (especially when the items began on a new line); however, in modern writing one seldom sees the hyphen used.

SECTION C   Same paper as used in Section A.

```
 1  Our train was late in arriving at Crewe; consequently, we missed you.
 2  The contents were as follows: Part I - Introduction; Part II - Practical.
 3  The castle looked splendid in the moonlight; the drawbridge was down.
 4  Profits are down; therefore, we must increase prices of all our products.
 5  The union's representative said: Obviously, the Works Manager is at fault.
 6  Please order the following: 2 typist's chairs, and 3 4-drawer cabinets.
 7  The Grand Imperial Hotel is excellent; clients return again and again.
 8  The computer cost a lot of money; accordingly, it should give good results.
```
